GW01607842

SCHOOLMA'AM TRUDY

SCHOOLMA'AM TRUDY

MARY ALICE FAID

LONDON

PICKERING & INGLIS LTD

PICKERING & INGLIS LTD.
29 Ludgate Hill, London, E.C.4
26 Bothwell Street, Glasgow, C.2
Home Evangel Books Ltd., 25 Hobson Avenue, Toronto, 16

SBN 7208 2029 4

First published - 1955
Reprinted - - 1959
" - - 1968

Printed in Great Britain

CONTENTS

CHAPTER I

GOODBYE TO COLLEGE

"IN about an hour's time," remarked Trudy as she pressed a wave into her red-gold hair, "you and I will be fully-fledged schoolma'ams. Doesn't the prospect scare you, Esther?"

"It does, a bit," confessed her room-mate. "Even the prospect of going up for my diploma under all those eyes scares me! Fortunately, my 'Moore' follows your 'Lawson' alphabetically, which means we will be sitting together."

A happy end, thought Trudy, to their three years at Martonbury, where she and her friend had stuck together through good times and bad. Hard work and discouragement there had been in plenty. But now they had both passed their finals with flying colours, and tomorrow they would say goodbye to college days for ever.

"Ready?" asked Trudy a few minutes later. "You do look lovely in white, Esther!" There was nothing Esther did not look lovely in. Her beauty of face and figure attracted attention wherever she went. Trudy knew that she herself would never be strictly beautiful. Though her hair was quite pretty, she had freckles and an unsatisfactory nose, but these were things one could not change, so why worry? Beauty was only skin deep after all, though Esther was an exception. Her kind of beauty was through and through. Now that their ways were about to part, she would miss her friend more than words could say.

Arm in arm they walked through the grounds of the college towards the lecture hall where the graduation ceremony was to take place. Seats had been reserved for them in front, along with the other students who were passing out.

As they filed in and sat there waiting they were already aware of the solemnity of the occasion. The hall was gradually filling, first with students, then with the friends and relations who had come specially for the event. Through the open windows Trudy could hear the cheerful song of thrush and blackbird, and the scent of roses was everywhere.

It was July and the sun shed its warm beams on the rows of white-clad girls who to-day were leaving college for a new life. A few years after this, thought Trudy, and where would they all be? Sometimes you felt you would do anything to be able to see into the future. But it might not be a good thing. Better to discover it as you went along, like an explorer. It was more exciting that way, more full of surprises.

They were sitting very still, eyes front, as was only proper, but she did wish she could turn round to see if the family had arrived yet. Esther's father was bringing them in his car, but she would not see them till after the ceremony. Her mother would be there, and Ping, her young brother, whose school was on holiday. Nancy, now a probationer in Drumleigh Hospital, might possibly manage too. As for David, the eldest, he was a very busy young man these days. Two years ago he had won a travelling scholarship at art school, and had been abroad for a whole year. At present he was a designer in a textile factory and it was not easy for him to get away.

"Things are beginning to happen at last," whispered Esther, as the door on the platform opened and the college staff, in gowns and mortar boards, came solemnly to take their places. There were other important people, too, including Sir Andrew Ross, Chairman of the College Board, and, of course, Miss Stratton, the Head.

The ceremony began with a hymn and a prayer. Then Sir Andrew, as chairman, began to give them a history of the college. It seemed a very long speech to the girls who were nervously waiting, and they were glad when Miss Stratton at last took his place.

In her first year Trudy had been rather in awe of the severe looking Head, but in time she had come to respect and understand her. To-day she listened intently to her farewell words, addressed to the departing students:

"This college has sheltered you for three years, has given you advice and helped you in the search for knowledge. Now it is your turn to help others. You are going out from here to teach the young. In your hands rests a big responsibility. Do not forget this, girls! And remember, too, the college motto: *Veritas Prevalebit*—'The Truth will prevail.'"

The girls cheered at the familiar words, but silence fell as the Head continued: "And now to proceed with the awarding of prizes and diplomas."

The moment had come at last. Esther caught Trudy's hand and held it fast. The 'A's came first, and as each girl stepped up to the platform, Miss Stratton made a few remarks about her progress, giving praise where it was due.

At last Trudy heard her own name and letting go Esther's hand forced herself to walk forward.

"Gertrude Lawson—awarded the Teaching Diploma, Special Prize for English Literature, and Gold Medal for best all-round student——" Her last words were drowned in a tumult of applause. Trudy wondered why they were all clapping so loudly. Her face was very pale as she stood before the smiling Head.

"Yes, Trudy, they are clapping for you, and you deserve it. Not only because you have worked hard; but you have been an inspiration to everyone in this college. May you go on to be a shining light in the career you have taken up!"

It was too much. Shining light, indeed. They would tease her about this at home! Oh dear, Miss Stratton was shaking her hand now, Sir Andrew, too. The noise below became deafening. Would they never stop?

They cheered again as she went back to her seat. And now it was Esther's turn. There was more enthusiastic applause as she was awarded her Diploma and Special Music Prize and complimented on her general prowess and behaviour.

"The college will be poorer without these two friends. They have had the courage, during their years here, to make Christianity a real live thing.

Though they are leaving, their influence will remain," announced Miss Stratton as Esther, pink-cheeked, stepped off the platform.

It was good to be seated again, out of the lime-light!

"How do you feel, Esther?"

"Terrible. Do you think she really meant us? We'll never be able to live up to this, Trudy!"

"We'll never be able to live it down, you mean!"

Now that their turn was over, they were able to relax. The end came with the singing of the college song, and then they were free at last to go and find their friends.

* * * * *

Trudy and Esther stepped out into the sunshine of the grassy sward studded with trees. In a twinkling they were confronted by a tall schoolboy in shorts and blazer who grinned widely:

"Hello, Shining Lights!"

"I knew it!" wailed Trudy. "Ping, if you call us that again, I'll pound you to a jelly!"

"Just try it," was the threat. "I'm strong—feel that muscle! Came in first at the school sports. Trudy, I'm going in for athletics. Did you know?"

Ping was no longer a small, freckled boy; nothing babyish about him now. He was growing up almost too fast, was actually at High School, learning —or supposed to be learning!—subjects like French and Latin.

"The others are over there, waiting for you."

The girls hurried over to join the group at the big oak tree. Trudy saw that besides her mother and Esther's father, Nancy was there too—yes, and David! He had not changed much since she saw him last, except to become, if possible, more good-looking. But Nancy had filled out and seemed to tower over her, though she was two years younger.

It was a sparkling reunion, with everybody speaking at once. Her mother's eyes were shining.

"Well, Trudy, this is the day you have lived for! I suppose you are very happy?"

"Very happy, Mum, and very grateful."

Years ago, when her father died, her dream of college had faded, and it had only been made possible again by the bequest of an old lady they had befriended. She would never forget Miss Primrose nor cease to be grateful to her.

"You're a real teacher now, I suppose," remarked Nancy. "Think of the years I've to go before I'm a real nurse!"

"If you're ever one," teased Ping. "I've heard you say that you'd never stick it."

Nancy frowned. Ping needn't bring that up now. True, there was no glamour about a probationer, and sometimes her duties got her down, but in her heart she was determined to 'stick it'. Trudy had been through hard times too, and here she was, top of the college, her ambitions realised.

"How did you manage to get away?" Trudy asked her brother.

David's eyes twinkled. "Special leave. Our factory has a branch in Martonbury; I've to see the manager this afternoon." But when she asked what about, he would not tell her. "Never mind that. The important thing is—congratulations, both!"

As he shook hands with Esther, Trudy saw a look of deep admiration on his face. She knew that her friend sometimes got letters from David, and she still had a little pansy brooch he had once given her. In fact, she was wearing it to-day and her cheeks were rosy as she smiled into his eyes.

Mr. Moore was regarding his daughter rather wistfully. Was he thinking that sometime in the future he might have to give her up to someone else? Trudy could see signs of age in his lined face and iron grey hair. His was the harrowing life of a city businessman, and he did not get much leisure.

Her reflections were interrupted by the advent of no less a person than Miss Stratton. She greeted them very amiably:

"Good afternoon! I'm very pleased to have this chance of speaking to the parents of our two star students. Trudy, my dear—" she laid a hand on her shoulder—"have you done anything about getting a teaching post after the holidays?"

"Well, I've sent in an application to the County Authority, Miss Stratton. I'd like to get a school in my home town Drumleigh."

"I see." Her tone was reflective. "I might be able to get you a better post, teaching English in a rather exclusive girls' school in Martonbury. Life would be much easier for you there; you would get full scope for your talents. Some town schools are rather rough for young teachers!"

"That's very kind of you," responded Trudy.

"If you make a good start in the right kind of school, you might go very high in the teaching profession. I'll write you very soon!" And she moved off in her stately way to join another group nearby.

"Oh, Trudy, how splendid!" exclaimed Esther. "I do hope you get the 'exclusive' school. You deserve it!"

Trudy was thrilled. "Sounds like a good chance to take my own subject. I don't know where I'd be if I got things like arithmetic to teach."

But Ping was getting impatient. "Hi, folks, is there any food around here? I'm starvishing!"

The little-boy expression brought a reminiscent smile. Mr. Moore then sprang a pleasant surprise. "I have booked a table for lunch at the Martonbury Hotel. How long will it take you to get ready, girls?"

"Two jiffies!" Esther caught Trudy's arm and raced her off to their room in the hostel. Breathlessly, they tidied their hair and got into their college blazers. Lunch out was a treat that seldom came their way.

High spirits prevailed as they sat round the table in the hotel dining room, Mr. Moore and Mrs. Lawson at either end, Ping beside Nancy, and David with Esther. Good company, and good food. After the plain college diet, the menu was most exciting: mushroom soup, delicious roast beef and greens, and a dessert that combined all Ping's favourites—meringue, fruit salad, ice-cream.

"I wish you two graduated every day!" he sighed as the last dainty morsel disappeared.

"If you got a lunch like that every day, you'd get as used to it as you are to porridge," said Nancy, to his disgust and disbelief.

* * * * *

Mr. Moore had to return to business and the others to their various tasks. When the party broke up, Trudy and Esther went back to college to pack their things for departure tomorrow. Some of these belongings had been with them for the whole three years of their stay. The green bedroom slippers Nancy had knitted for Trudy were on their last lap, with a hole in each toe.

"I really ought to throw them out, but they've got what you call 'sentimental value'. I'll mend them and take them with me to the exclusive school."

"And your picture," said Esther. "Don't forget that!"

Trudy took it down from the wall, the painting David had done three years ago of the family in the garden. "How young Ping looks! Nancy, too. She used to be so untidy, but she's improved a lot, hasn't she, Esther? Mum is just the same. She'll always be the same."

Esther looked over her shoulder at the sweet, smiling face. Trudy was right. Mrs. Lawson had something about her that did not wear off with time—a look of sympathy and loving kindness that gave a shine to her features and endeared her to all.

"I'll take this picture with me wherever I go,

Esther. Even when I'm a withered old head mistress."

"You'll never be withered! And you'll never be a head mistress, either, I believe. You're sure to get married before long."

"Married? Never!" No such thought had entered her head. "What would be the good of all those years at college? No, I'm a career girl. It's you that will get married, Esther."

Her friend blushed. "Why, who would want to marry me?"

Trudy smiled. "I could give a good guess!"

"I don't know what you mean," replied Esther, turning to her packing. The subject was dropped, but as she studied the pensive profile, Trudy thought how thrilling it would be if her guess came true. Then Esther would be her sister-in-law. But a lot was bound to happen before then; she must put it out of her mind.

"Remember the first night we came here, how lonely and far from home we felt?" she asked, as the packing went on. "We read that bit from the Bible, 'If I take the wings of the morning and dwell in the uttermost parts of the sea, even then shall Thy hand lead me'."

"Yes, I remember. How it comforted us! What shall we read tonight?"

"I like the Psalms best," said Trudy. "Which one is it that speaks of 'My rock and my fortress'?"

Esther had a good memory. "The thirty-first."

So they spent part of their last evening in college

reading from the Book which had been their inspiration during those studious years.

"In Thee, O Lord, do I put my trust . . . for Thou art my rock and my fortress: therefore for Thy Name's sake, lead me and guide me." The future was uncertain for them, as for everyone, especially now they were setting out on new paths. But whatever happened, they would always have that 'rock and fortress' to give them strength.

CHAPTER II

AN ACCIDENT TO PING

NEXT day they said goodbye to Martonbury. It was not only the college they were sorry to leave. During their three years there Trudy and Esther had been active workers in Dene's Court Mission, run by the Crawford family. Last Sunday they had taken leave of Mr. Crawford and his son, Derek.

"I hope it's only *au revoir,*" the latter had said in farewell. They promised that they would come back, if only for a visit.

"If you get that post Miss Stratton spoke about," remarked Esther as their train left Martonbury station, "you'll be back here in a month or two. Then you will be seeing more of the Crawfords. Theirs is such a welcoming house!"

Recalling the pleasant Sundays they had spent there, Trudy agreed whole-heartedly. "But I'll not count on it, Esther. Perhaps Miss Stratton will forget all about me."

Meanwhile, she was only too happy to be going home again.

She found only two people in the house—her mother and Ping. He was getting ready to go off for a fortnight's camping with the school to Seathorpe. Ever since their island holiday at Ardensheel, he had longed to live in a tent again. It was the first time he had been away alone, and Trudy realised anew that he was growing up. They were all growing up.

"In no time your youngest will be a man. What will you do when you have no children left?" she asked her mother, as they helped an excited Ping to don his bulging haversack.

"You will always be children to me," replied Mrs. Lawson, "and of course I hope to have grandchildren some day! Ping, you will write to us, won't you? I've put some stamped letter-cards in for you."

"Of course I'll write. But don't expect long lingos like Trudy's! We'll have our chores to do, and us big boys will have to look after the little ones." He spoke with an air of grown-upness that amused them.

Trudy said she would accompany him to the station, but first Ping must call in next door to say goodbye.

It was five years ago now since the Drysdales had come to stay there, and four years since Stephen Drysdale had married Trudy's English teacher, Miss Forsyth. Now they had a baby daughter, Bunty, with whom Ping was a firm favourite. She was in her mother's arms to-day, making a lovely picture at the door. Mrs. Drysdale offered Trudy sincere congratulations:

"I knew you could do it, Trudy! You were always my best English pupil. Well, Ping, so you're off to camp. Take care of yourself, you're precious, you know! Isn't he, Bunty?" The baby smiled, holding out her arms to him.

"I can't nurse you just now," explained her hero,

"but we'll play lots of games when I come home!"

They were halfway to the station when he suddenly exclaimed: "Oh, look, there's Rusty, and I thought I'd given him the slip!" His dog, a brown corgi, came tearing along the road, barking noisily, to throw himself joyfully upon him.

"Home, Rusty!" he commanded.

Poor Rusty could hardly believe that he was not wanted. He stood looking after them sadly, before he turned disconsolately homeward.

"Why can't a boy go away without feeling sad?" demanded Ping. "I just hate goodbyes, don't you?"

Trudy agreed that goodbyes were depressing, no matter for how short a time. Ping's spirit's returned, however, when they reached the station and he met his schoolmates, a cheerful, chattering crowd.

Waving to her from the carriage window, he looked the happiest boy on earth, bubbling over with the joy of life. Yet, with the last look she had of him as the train disappeared, she seemed to catch a glimpse of the old Ping, the sweet little boy, thoughtful for others, implicitly believing in the power of love and goodness. It was odd how loth she was to let him go. But, she reminded herself, it was only for a fortnight, and he needed this holiday. For herself, home was a holiday. She would keep house later on and let her mother and Nancy go away somewhere together.

* * * * *

That night she and her mother were alone, as David was working late and Nancy, of course, lived in at the hospital. As she wandered through the empty rooms recalling old memories, she thought how different it all was from the old days when Dad was here and the four of them were at school. Then, there had been six people to cook and wash for, six cups on the table, six pairs of slippers at the fire.

"I don't know how you can stand it!" she exclaimed impulsively.

Her mother looked up from her sewing: "Stand what, Trudy?"

"This awful silence, when there used to be such goings on!"

Mrs. Lawson laughed. "But things can't stay the same way for ever. Every phase of life has its compensations, Trudy. It's a bit dull just now, but not for long."

Trudy took a favourite footstool at her feet. "You take things so calmly, Mum. You seem to be ready for any emergency."

A gentle hand was laid on Trudy's sunny hair. "You know my secret, dear."

"Yes, Mum." Through years of joy and sorrow, her mother's faith in God's goodness had never faltered. Her faith was also Trudy's, but being young, she had her moments of questioning, even of rebellion. Why couldn't one stay happy? Why did troubles have to come? She was also a little impatient about the future. The days seemed long, waiting for Miss Stratton to write her, and she missed Esther, who had gone abroad with her father and would not be back for some time. A glowing letter came from her, telling of all the wonders of foreign travel.

"I wish you were here, too, Trudy! We stayed a few nights in Paris—can you imagine it? Some day when we are both schoolma'ams, we'll have our holidays together, so polish up your French!" She went on to ask if there had been any news of the 'exclusive school'. "A school like that would suit me fine. I'd hate to have to deal with an unruly mob! How are all the family? Give them my love, or as many of them as are at home."

The letter was on the mantelpiece when David came in, and he immediately recognised the writing.

"Hello, is that from Esther?"

"You can read it if you like," Trudy told him.

He lost no time doing so, and she saw him take a note of the address, but said nothing. David hated to be teased.

They were in the room alone and David took the opportunity to say: "Trudy, I want to ask your advice about something."

She was pleasantly surprised. Her brother seemed to have grown so old and self-sufficient lately.

"I'll help you if I can, David."

"Well, you know I went to see the manager of the Martonbury factory that day? It's a much more modern place than ours and their designer gets quite a good salary; but he's leaving them soon."

He paused, and she asked: "You mean, you are applying for his job?"

"Not exactly, I don't need to apply. The job has been offered me."

"Oh, David, how wonderful!"

"I haven't accepted yet, though. I'd love it, of course. For one thing, the hours are shorter and I'd have time to do some real painting. Then I'd be able to save something for—well, a chap might get married some day, you know." He had the grace to blush.

Trudy smiled. "Quite right, David. Why don't you snap up the job, then? I don't understand."

"Well, you see, I'd have to live in Martonbury. That would mean Mum would be more alone than ever."

"Yes, there's that." Trudy pondered. "But I don't think she would mind. Ping will be at home and Nancy very near. Besides, I might not get that 'exclusive school' and would be staying at home myself."

"You really think I ought to accept, then?" he asked eagerly.

"Definitely. Mention it to Mum tonight, and you'll see she'll agree."

Trudy was right. Mrs. Lawson was delighted that David was considered competent enough for the new job. She was not the one to stand in his way, and urged him to settle the matter at once.

"After all, Martonbury is only fifty miles away and you will get home some week-ends. When will you have to start?"

"Next week," he admitted. "Will you come through with me on Saturday to look for digs, Mum?"

"Certainly. You, too, Trudy?"

Trudy decided, however, to stay at home. She had had enough of Martonbury for the present.

* * * * *

Not long after David and his mother left the house on Saturday, the post brought three letters. Though curious about the other two, Trudy opened Ping's first. It was a hasty scrawl, giving an exuberant account of camp life, with words misspelled and periods missed out, but that was to be expected. Putting it aside to re-read again, she opened the second letter. Miss Stratton had not forgotten her promise. The communication was from St. Bride's School, Martonbury, offering Trudy the post of English mistress to the junior girls, as she had been so highly recommended by the Head of the college. Would she let them know her decision as soon as possible?

St. Bride's! It was a top-grade boarding school with picked pupils, and had the loveliest situation imaginable. Life would be very pleasant there. She would get inspiration to write poetry, as she had always longed to do. She was so thrilled by the prospect that it was some time before she remembered about the other letter.

Not so exciting, this one. It was a short note from the County Authority. At the moment there were no openings for a beginner to teach English exclusively, but an elementary teacher to take all subjects was required in Balfour Street School, Drumleigh. Later, she might be posted to something better. Would she let them know?

Balfour Street was down in the crowded part of the town and the children, she knew, were rather wild. A tough proposition for a new teacher! But, of course, there was no question about her going there. Who would choose a school like Balfour Street when you could go to St. Bride's?

Having done her household duties, her thoughts in a glow, she sat down with the best writing paper to pen two notes. The one to the Authority, declining their offer, was easy. But she was so anxious to make the other one perfect, her nerves caused her to make mistakes, and she tore up her first two attempts. She was just beginning a third, when she heard a heavy step at the door and put down her pen to answer a loud ring.

Bewildered, she saw before her a very large policeman.

"Name of Lawson?" he asked. "Is your mother in?"

"No," she told him, her mother was away for the day.

He looked perturbed. "Well, I'll have to give you the message, Miss. It's bad news about the boy—your brother, is he, that's camping at Seathorpe?"

"Yes," she faltered. "Ping. His right name's Peter. What has happened to him?"

"Steady on," he bade her, coming into the hall. "You must keep calm. You'll have to take your mother's place. The boy has had an accident—climbed down a cliff to rescue a smaller lad. Brave thing to do, but he's badly hurt."

Trudy gripped the hallstand in an effort to steady herself. "Is he—won't he—get better?"

"Now, now, lass, don't jump to the worst," was the kindly reply. "Boys are tough mortals. His master phoned the police station. He wanted Mrs. Lawson to go straight to Seathorpe. Pity she's away. Can't you get in touch with her?"

Trudy shook her head. "I'm afraid not. But I'll go to Seathorpe myself and leave a note here for her."

The constable was most helpful and waited by while she wrote the note and got ready. Then he went with her to the station. Seathorpe was only an hour's journey and there was a train almost immediately. He saw her on to it and gave her the address of the hospital where they had taken Ping.

"If you don't get home tonight, phone us and we'll get in touch with your mother. Keep your pecker up, lass! It might not be so bad."

She did her best to smile as the train moved out. It had all happened so quickly she'd had no time to think. But now, alone in the compartment, there was nothing else to do. Poor Ping—she could still hear his voice saying: "Us big boys will have to look after the little ones!" He simply would not think of his own danger at all.

The journey seemed endless, but here was Seathorpe at last. She knew it well—a lovely place with cliffs and sands and everything to make one happy. The sun was shining and everyone looked so jolly and carefree. How could they, when such a terrible thing had happened to Ping?

In the waiting room of the hospital, she was met by Mr. Graham, Ping's schoolmaster, his usually cheerful face drawn with anxiety.

"We don't know yet how serious it is, Miss Lawson," he told her. "But I'll be frank with you—he's pretty bad."

"What happened exactly?" Trudy asked shakily.

"Well, one of the smaller boys went down the cliff to look for a rock pigeon's nest, and was stranded on a ledge. He got very excited and would probably have gone over, but your brother climbed down beside him till the others got a rope. The wee chap was got up safely, but then part of the ledge crumbled away, and Ping——"

She shivered. "I see——"

"Sit down, Miss Lawson, you're very pale. What a pity your mother couldn't come! You look so young to have a shock like this."

"I'm all right," she assured him. "I'm older than I look, really."

At last, after what seemed hours, the matron of the hospital called them to her room. Two doctors were there, looking very grave. Ping's main injuries, they said, were to his back. He would not be able to move for a very long time. And perhaps he would never walk again.

Not walk! Ping, who had never been able to stay still for two minutes, to whom action was his very life. How would he be able to bear it? And what was Mum going to say when she heard?

"Miss Lawson—" very gently Mr. Graham led her away—"you have been very brave up till now.

Your mother will need you, and so will Ping. Can you go on being brave?"

Trudy's head went up and she gave him a clear, straightforward glance. "I'll do my best, Mr. Graham!"

Her best! How very little that was! But fortunately she was not alone. Though her own strength might fail, that 'rock and fortress' was still there, whatever might befall.

CHAPTER III

A SCHOOL FOR TRUDY

BEFORE she went back home that day, Trudy visited the hospital again with Mr. Graham and was allowed to see Ping for a few minutes. He was in a little bed at the end of the ward, lying so still you would think there was no life in him. The nurse explained that he was encased in a plaster jacket, to keep him from moving about.

"Is he asleep?" whispered Trudy. But at the sound of her voice Ping opened his eyes. There was a faraway look in them that went to her heart. Then, seeing his lips move, she bent forward.

"Hello, True." Faint as an echo, the words.

"Hello, Ping! Don't try to talk. I'm here beside you."

"I fell——" he said slowly. You could see he was trying to remember. "Is the wee boy all right?"

She assured him that the boy whose life he had saved was quite well and happy, and was rewarded with the shadow of a smile. Then his eyes closed again and his long lashes lay motionless on his cheeks.

"Don't worry about him. He's a plucky little lad and will win through," counselled the nurse.

But her heart was very heavy. As there was no point in staying at Seathorpe any longer, she took the train home and was in time to greet her mother and David when they got back. They looked very happy, both of them, which made it all the harder to break the news.

Her mother took it bravely, however. No matter how grief-stricken she felt, Mrs. Lawson was always able to school her feelings.

"I'm glad you were able to see him, Trudy. You did the right thing, going to Seathorpe. I'll go straight there first thing tomorrow and stay as long as he needs me. I know I can trust you to look after things here."

"I can't believe it!" proclaimed David. "If it were anyone but Ping! He was so full of life. Lately he's been going in for athletics, too. He wanted to be a runner, even talked about going in for the Olympic Games some day! Tough on him, poor kid."

"We'll just have to keep him going with our love," murmured his mother, "and trust that some day he may be able to get about again."

"There was a letter from him this morning, and he was so full of vim!" Trudy found it for her mother, and mentioned the other two letters she had received and which had not yet been answered. Could it only have been this morning they arrived? How happy she had been then, at the prospect of going to St. Bride's!

"But this changes everything, of course. I couldn't go to Martonbury and leave you, Mum. With Ping in hospital, you would be alone most of the time."

"Pity I accepted that new job," observed David sadly.

"You are not to think of me," replied his mother.

"Trudy, you mustn't give up this fine chance. You may never get another like it."

But Trudy was sure she would not be happy, so far away from her mother and Ping.

"Wait for a day or two," advised Mrs. Lawson. "You must take time to consider. I think you should go to bed now, Trudy, you look tired. But first, we'll have the Bible reading."

Ever since Trudy remembered they had held a short service at bedtime. When they were all at home, they had sung hymns which Nancy accompanied on the piano. Tonight there were only the three of them and they did not feel like singing, so David read the Twenty-third Psalm, his voice faltering at the words, "Yea, though I walk through the valley of the shadow of death, I will fear no evil: for Thou art with me——" Ping loved his Bible and knew so much of it by heart. Would the memory of these words be comforting him now, as he lay so still in his narrow bed?

They knelt to pray and Mrs. Lawson commended her young son to God's keeping. It was all they could do for Ping at the moment, to pray for him and keep on praying. That there was no limit to the power of prayer was Mrs. Lawson's firm belief.

Out of sheer exhaustion Trudy slept at last, but she had to be up early to see her mother off to Seathorpe, and David was obliged to go to his work as usual. Yesterday's search for lodgings had been successful and they had engaged a room in a house near his new job.

It was Saturday, and in the afternoon Nancy came

home for the week-end, and had to be told what had happened. In her impulsive way, she wanted to rush straight off to Seathorpe too.

"But you can't do Ping any good, Nancy. He won't want anyone but Mum. Stay here with me, please. You've no idea how empty this house seems when you're alone in it!"

"Of course I'll stay." Nancy gave her a hug. "Only, I want to *do* something—not just reading or sewing as I usually do. What about us cleaning the attic? I heard Mum say it was needing a tidy-up."

It certainly seemed a good way to keep one from thinking. Armed with brush and mop they climbed the ladder into the big attic where they used to spend their leisure hours, David at his modelling and painting, Nancy playing the violin and Trudy trying to write poetry. One corner was Ping's, and here they found his old playthings—the model village, crumbling to pieces, the clockwork train rusty and broken. Nancy sniffed tearfully as she picked it up.

"I'd give a thousand pounds to see him playing with this again!"

Poor Nancy, she hadn't a thousand pennies, let alone pounds.

"But he's too old for it, anyway. Cheer up, Nancy, he'll play again, I'm sure of it. What about giving us a tune on the violin?"

"It's ages since I tried it, but I'll have a go if you like." She tuned up the old instrument and began to play all Ping's favourite tunes. They laughed at some of them and cried at others. Music had such power to bring back memories!

"But this isn't getting on with the job." Nancy returned the violin to its case. "Come along, all hands on deck!"

The clean-up took a very long time, for they were always coming on some reminder of the past. A 'head' of Esther—one of the many which David had modelled—and fragments of dried-up clay; a notebook of Trudy's with some poems which she had thought quite good at the time but which now seemed very poor; torn pages of music and a lot of 'pure rubbish' as Nancy termed it. It was hard work clearing out the useless things, sweeping and scrubbing, but at the end they both felt much calmer in mind.

* * * * *

Mrs. Lawson did not come home that night, so Trudy knew that she had found a place to stay and was glad she would be near Ping. On Monday they got a letter from her. Ping was very low. He had hardly spoken, not even to ask what was wrong with him or how long he would be in hospital.

"It will have to be kept from him that he may never walk again. However, there is one bit of comforting news. After a time he can be nursed at home, if we can give him the necessary attention. And we can, can't we, girls?"

"Of course we can!" exclaimed Nancy. "I'll devote all my free time to him. After all, I do know something about nursing."

"And I'll write to St. Bride's at once, telling them I can't come," stated Trudy.

"Oh, but True! Isn't it just the very thing you wanted?"

"Yes, but the family comes first." She had definitely made up her mind.

"You'll just hate that scruffy old school in Balfour Street!"

"Perhaps," she said wistfully. "But sometimes things turn out better than you expect. I'll get home every day at four and that's something."

"It seems to me you're always giving up things you want! There was that time you went as governess, when Dad died and we hadn't any money."

"Well, that turned out all right, didn't it? I got to college after all. Mum says that God's plans are better than ours, though it's hard to see it sometimes!" And she sighed, for she would dearly have loved St. Bride's and it cost her a lot to write that letter of refusal.

At the same time, she penned a note to Miss Stratton, thanking her for her recommendation and explaining her reasons for not accepting the post. Back came an expression of regret from the college Head.

"I am so sorry to hear about your brother's accident, and I appreciate your action, Trudy. It is just the sort of thing a girl like you would do, and it is not for me to say you are wrong. Would your friend Esther Moore care to be considered for the vacant post? Next to you, she would suit St. Bride's admirably."

Trudy lost no time in replying, for she knew that Esther would be keen. The day after she came home from abroad, she had a visit from her. It was a warm, sunny afternoon, Mrs. Lawson was still at Seathorpe and Trudy was in the house alone. She saw Esther from the window, looking very summery in a blue nylon frock and shady hat. Esther had been living in a gayer, brighter world, but she knew that would make no difference to their friendship. Arm in arm, they went to talk in the summerhouse at the back. How many secrets that old summerhouse had overheard!

"Trudy, darling, I can't tell you how sorry Dad and I are about Ping. How is he?"

"No different, I'm afraid. Mum says he's very quiet and sad; she can't rouse him at all. Soon we'll be getting him home, though. Have you heard from St. Bride's, Esther?"

She nodded. "The letter was waiting for me at home. Trudy, I hate taking this post when it ought to be yours!"

Trudy understood her feelings. "But, Esther, I'd rather it went to you than anybody. We could write to each other and compare notes. 'Lady Esther' from the exclusive boarding school, to plain Miss Lawson in Balfour Street. That's where the Authority is going to send me. You with your fine ladies and me with my rag-tag and bob-tail!"

"You would make a joke of it, of course. We'd have to make a point of meeting sometimes."

"Sure. It ought to be easy. And there's David, of course. I think I wrote you that he had a job in Martonbury?"

"Yes. How does he like it?"

"Very much. And I guess he will like it even better if you go there. Think of it, you'll be able to see him quite often."

"In a girls' boarding school?" Esther laughed. "Perhaps he'll disown me altogether. But if you really want me to, Trudy, I'll go to St. Bride's if they'll have me."

So it was arranged, and the appointment made.

* * * * *

The summer holidays wore on, and Trudy duly took her mother's place at Seathorpe for a week or two, getting the benefit of the sea breezes in the forenoons and visiting Ping after lunch every day. She read to him and told him stories, but he showed very little interest. It seemed as if the main part of Ping, his bright, responsive self, had fled for ever, and she was worried and sad.

At length it was arranged for Ping to get home in a week's time, as an experiment. It was the only thing, said the doctor, that might bring him back to life again.

Trudy brought the news home to her mother. "It will mean a lot of work for you, Mum, but Nancy and I will help. We'll organise the house to make it as easy as possible. We'll have to keep him downstairs, for one thing. What about Miss Primrose's room?"

The small back room had not been used for anything special since Miss Primrose, the 'paying guest', had occupied it. It was rather a dull little room and had not been decorated for years.

"I know!" she went on. "We'll do it up for him. Nancy and I can sew curtains and things and David can do the walls. Wouldn't it be grand if he could paint some murals!"

David came home for the week-end and set to work, while Nancy and Trudy took turn about at the sewing machine.

Soon the room was transformed. Besides a small bed, a sofa had been brought in with big cushions whose covers matched the rose pink curtains. The fireplace and doors were apple green, the shade of the rug at the bedside. Ping's books and playthings were put in a cupboard near the bed, and cheerful vases of flowers were set round the room.

But the most delightful feature was David's murals. All round the walls he painted in bright, arresting colours, the Bible scenes which would best appeal to the invalid. On one wall was a picture of Jesus with a little child, just like Bunty next door, and underneath the text: 'Suffer little children to come unto me'. Opposite, the Master was healing the blind beggar, and on another wall was a wonderful depiction of the lad with the loaves and fishes which were to feed the Five Thousand.

"Oh, David, Ping will love them!" Trudy gazed at his handiwork admiringly.

"I hope he will. I'd do more than that to make him happy!"

The big day came, and Mrs. Lawson went to Seathorpe to bring Ping home. Trudy stood at the gate waiting for the ambulance to arrive. She was joined by young Mrs. Drysdale.

"It won't seem so bad when you've got him home," remarked her neighbour. "You'll be able to do things for him."

"There's nothing we wouldn't do," said Trudy simply. "I only hope it isn't too much for Mum."

"Not with two such daughters as you and Nancy! You must be feeling bad about giving up the St. Bride's post, Trudy."

"Not if it does any good, Mrs. Drysdale."

"You won't find Balfour Street a refined school by any means, but a teacher's job always has compensations. If you have any problems, I hope you will consult me, Trudy. I know the snags a young teacher comes up against."

Trudy knew the words were sincere. "Thank you," she said. "I'll have lots of problems, I know."

Then their attention was distracted by the appearance of a large ambulance coming along the road and stopping at the gate. Ping had come home. A different Ping from the boy who had gaily stepped out a few weeks ago. But it would not do to think about that now. They must keep smiling for his sake, make his homecoming a bright and happy thing. Not by their own power could they do it. Now if ever they would need that extra strength which only prayer could bring.

CHAPTER IV

TRUDY'S FIRST DAY

PING was brought into the house on a stretcher borne by two kindly ambulance men and laid in the bed which was ready waiting for him.

Trudy stood beside him, sad in her heart to see his cheeks so pale, his smile so listless. She took his thin hand in hers.

"Welcome home, Ping! We've put you in Miss Primrose's room, so that we can be near you all the time. How do you like the improvements?"

"They're nice," he replied, but she realised with a pang that he was not really interested.

"David painted the murals. Aren't they lovely?"

"Yes, I think so, but I can't see them properly." He was lying on his back, as he would have to do for a very long time to come.

"We'll have to get him to paint some pictures on the ceiling, like some of the big buildings in Italy. Esther told me about them. She's just home from abroad."

"Is she? I'd like to go to Italy. But I'll never go anywhere, now."

She could see his lip trembling, though he bit it stoically.

"Oh, come, Ping, you'll see the world yet. It seems a long time to be ill, but think of the years and years ahead."

"That's what I'm doing." A sigh broke from him.

"Years and years of lying in bed. It's no use, Trudy! You're keeping it from me, but I know."

Her heart ached for him. "Ping, don't talk like that. You're going to be walking about in no time!"

He gave a sad little laugh. "I'm not a baby, so you might as well tell me the truth."

She tried to reassure him. There was a chance, she admitted, that he might not wholly recover, but she and her mother—the doctors, too—thought there was just as good a chance of complete cure.

"Thanks for saying it, anyway, Trudy. I suppose this serves me right in a way, for boasting about being so strong. Remember, I was going in for athletics?"

"Yes, Ping, but one of the most famous athletes of Britain was a very sick boy once. They said he would never run again, yet he won ever so many championships."

"You mean Eric Liddell? But he was different. Sorry, Trudy! I'll try not to grumble. I'm going to be a big enough burden without that."

"Nonsense," she returned. "You know the story about the wee girl who was carrying a baby far too big for her? 'That's a heavy burden you've got,' somebody said to her, but she just answered: 'It's not a burden, it's my brother!'" She tucked the clothes round him. "We love you too much for you to be a burden! Now I'll bring you something to eat. Mum's getting it ready."

Ping could not feed himself. He had an invalid cup with a spout like a teapot and a special tray that fitted over the bed, but his appetite was painfully small.

As the days went on and he showed no interest even in his food, they would have given anything to hear him use again that childhood expression, "I'm starvishing!"

The whole life of the house came to be centred in that little room. The minute any of the family came home, they went straight to Ping's bedside to relate all that had happened since they saw him last. In the evenings, Mrs. Lawson sewed or knitted beside him and Trudy read to him, while the family wireless set was brought in for his benefit.

He was very quiet and undemanding. Too undemanding! The old Ping would have torn the house apart, almost, to get what he wanted, but this new one just lay there, hour after hour, his natural high spirits vanished, it seemed, for ever.

Trudy would have begun her teaching career with a lighter heart if she could have seen even a flicker of his old self, but when the day came for her to start at the school in Balfour Street, Ping was no better. Now he would be more alone, with more time to brood.

"Never mind," she cheered him before leaving, "I'll have lots to tell you when I come home!"

She was all strung up for what lay ahead—her first day as a fully fledged teacher with a class of her own. What would the conditions at Balfour Street be? Would the other teachers be friendly, the children willing to be taught? She would soon know.

Though she arrived early at the school, some children were already in the playground. Seeing her, they got into a group and eyed her curiously. "It's the new teacher!" she heard them say. "Her?" came the reply. "She's only a lassie!" Oh, dear, was that how they were going to regard her?

With heightened colour she passed into the school. It was an old building, three storeys high, and the classrooms opened off from balconies built round a central hall. She found the headmaster's room, knocked, and at his bidding went in. Mr. Morison was a tall, thin man with spectacles and a long, scholarly face.

"So you are Miss Lawson. Well, I am glad to see you, as we are very short staffed. Though I do wish they had sent me someone with more experience. You look very young."

"I'm twenty-one," she told him.

He smiled. "And isn't that young? Wait till you're fifty, like me. Teaching here isn't easy, Miss Lawson. The pupils are difficult to manage."

"I don't mind that," she declared.

His eyebrows went up. "Well said, Miss Lawson! But we'll not be too hard on you to begin with. You can take class 5G. They are girls, not very bright, but well enough behaved. Just come this way."

As they went into the corridor, he called to a teacher who was passing: "Miss Bone, will you take charge of Miss Lawson, please? I am giving her your class of girls and would like you to take 5B instead."

She was a small, dried up woman with wispy

grey hair and a prim face. At his words, she frowned.

"5B? I don't care for boys, Mr. Morison. But if you say so——"

"I'm sure you can handle them . . . It wouldn't be fair to give that lot to a beginner, would it?"

She looked at Trudy sourly, then took her along to the lady teachers' staff room, and Trudy was confronted with about a dozen teachers all looking very much older and more experienced than herself.

"This is Miss Lawson, fresh from college." Miss Bone's voice was very dry as she made introductions.

"She won't be fresh long!" laughed one. "Not in this school!"

Trudy felt rather ill at ease. Through no fault of her own she seemed to have got into Miss Bone's bad books. Then one of the staff, a rosy cheeked person called Miss Kennedy, gave her a warm handshake.

"Balfour Street's not so bad, Miss Lawson, and please do keep fresh. We need someone young here to shake us up a bit!"

Trudy felt very grateful to her. She was going to need a friend like this.

Miss Bone then escorted her to a classroom on the second floor, showed her where to find register and timetable and gave her instructions in a clipped voice.

"Thank you," said Trudy. "I'm sorry you've had to give up your class. I wouldn't have minded taking those boys——"

"Wouldn't you? You don't know them," sniffed

the other. "What do you know about teaching, a girl like you?"

"I can learn," she said quietly. "And I did have a good training at college."

With another sniff, Miss Bone left her. Then the bell rang and in no time a line of schoolgirls filed into the room and she was subjected to curious glances as they went to their seats. She was glad to see that Mr. Morison had come in too.

"Good morning, girls!"

They stood to attention. "Good morning, sir!"

"This is your new teacher, Miss Lawson." He went on to say a few words about attention and discipline and then she was left alone in front of the class of forty girls.

The first lesson on the timetable was a Scripture one with a set passage from the Bible about the Parable of the Sower. No subject could have suited her better and she soon got their attention. Though not particularly bright, the girls seemed easy to manage and she was confident she would get on well with them.

The arithmetic lesson was not quite so successful. "Please, miss," they kept on telling her, "that's not the way Miss Bone does it!" Everything she did seemed to be different from Miss Bone, whose methods were old and out of date.

Four o'clock came at last. It had been a long day and she felt absolutely tired out. Yet this was only Monday. Four more days to go before Saturday!

As she was leaving the school, she heard a voice at her side.

"I hope you're not too discouraged with your first day, Miss Lawson?" It was Miss Kennedy.

"I didn't expect it to be easy," replied Trudy. "I only wish——"

"I know. You wish Miss Bone was a little more friendly?"

Trudy flushed. "What has she got against me, Miss Kennedy?"

"She is annoyed at having to take that class of boys, my dear. But perhaps her chief grudge is that you are young."

"But that's not my fault! She was young herself, once, wasn't she?"

"Undoubtedly," laughed the other. "But some of us maiden ladies forget that. We are jealous of young folk, and that makes us nasty to them."

It was a new thought for Trudy. "But you are not like that, Miss Kennedy."

"I try not to be. I think it a great privilege to be in the company of young people and to get their point of view. Besides, age has its compensations. But Miss Bone has shut herself off from young folk. Poor soul, she lives with her invalid mother, a very 'cranky' old person, indeed. In fact, she even gave up the chance of marriage to look after her."

"Did she really? Then she can't be so bad. I'll have to remember that."

* * * * *

At home, her mother was waiting eagerly to hear about her day.

"It wasn't so bad, Mum. The headmaster is nice and one of the teachers is a friend, already. There's a Miss Bone, though—but we'll forget about that. How is Ping?"

"Longing to see you."

Trudy went straight to Ping's room, feeling a new pang at sight of his pale, listless face.

"How long you've been, Trudy! I thought you were never coming home!"

"Never mind, I'm here now." With his hand in hers, she told him some of her adventures.

"I used to think school was horrid," remarked Ping, "but I'd give a lot to be able to go there now. It would be better than being stuck here all the time!"

"But, Ping, you don't need to be 'stuck' here. Your body, yes, but what about that imagination of yours? It can take you places." She suddenly had an idea. "Let's have a game of hide-and-seek!"

"Don't be silly," said her brother fretfully.

"Listen. Shut your eyes and imagine you're hiding in some place in the house or the garden. Then I'll guess where you are. Go on, Ping, it will be fun!"

Ping closed his eyes and after a moment, said: "All right, I'm hiding. Where am I?"

Trudy guessed the summer house, the kitchen cupboard, under the big room table—but it was none of them, so she gave up.

"I'm up on the washing-house roof!" declared Ping. "I can see the road with all the boys playing and lots of trees and hills, and big clouds rushing across the sky——" Slowly he opened his eyes again and there was a flicker of excitement in them.

"Trudy, I almost really *was* there! Now you shut your eyes and I'll guess."

They played at the new game till tea was ready. In his mind Ping visited all his old haunts and when his mother came in, he said eagerly:

"Do you know what, Mum? My imagination has legs! They can go ever so fast. I think I'll take a visit to Seathorpe tonight."

For the first time, he had an appetite for his meal. "Bless you for thinking up that game," said Mrs. Lawson that night. "It's going to make such a difference to Ping! He seems brighter already."

CHAPTER V

TRUDY WINS THE FIRST ROUND

ESTHER came round that night to say goodbye, for she was going to Martonbury next day. She was anxious to hear how Trudy had got on at Balfour Street School on her first day.

"Well!"—when the tale came to an end—"It doesn't sound like the kind of school you should be teaching in at all."

"Somebody's got to teach there," said Trudy philosophically.

"That Bone woman sounds absolutely horrid!"

"She seems to dislike me, Esther. You see, her class of girls was given to me and she had to take some very wild boys. The headmaster thinks I wouldn't be able to manage them, but I'd like to have a go!"

"I believe you've got the nerve for anything."

Trudy laughed. "Well, I'd love to overcome Miss Bone's prejudices. She might even come to like me. She's not all bad, you know."

"Nobody is, in your estimation," declared Esther. "Well, it will be my turn tomorrow. I hope there's not a Miss Bone at St. Bride's! I'm going to miss you, Trudy," her voice solemn.

"And I you, Esther."

"Trudy, will you go and see my father sometimes? I'm worried about him. He works so hard and doesn't seem well at all." There was a pucker on her high, white forehead.

Trudy promised to keep in touch. "I'll get Mum to ask your father for lunch on Sundays, if he will come."

"I'm sure it will be good for him. Benny, my brother, wants him to take a holiday at the farm, but he says he can't afford the time."

Trudy had almost forgotten that Esther had a brother, for he was seldom at home. Having taken an agricultural course, he now had a farm of his own which occupied all his time.

"Families do get broken up, don't they?" said Esther wistfully.

"Yes, but they needn't drift apart. I always think that even if all we Lawsons lived in different places, our real home would still be here. The minute David and Nancy are free, back they come, like homing pigeons."

"That's because of your mother. I feel like a homing pigeon myself when I come here! And now I must fly off."

The moment of parting had come. At the door they kissed each other with a rush of affection. The bond between them was more than ordinary friendship. Years ago at school they had taken together the great decision which had shaped their days and given them an ideal to live for.

Older now, they still thought of Jesus Christ as their Captain. With Him in command of their lives, steering them aright, nothing could go wrong, even in the roughest weather.

"We'll both go on fighting for the right, won't we, Trudy?"

"Harder now than ever. Bless you, Esther, and come back and see us soon."

* * * * *

Next morning, Trudy needed all her courage to enter the ladies' staff room. Several of the teachers smiled and said "Good morning," but the redoubtable Miss Bone, with hardly a glance, rose and made a dignified exit from the room.

Trudy flushed. "Did I send her out?" she asked Miss Kennedy.

"It looks like it, but don't let it worry you, Miss Lawson."

"No, indeed," said the outspoken gym mistress, Miss Austin. "No one worries about Boney. We leave her to come out of her moods the way she went into them."

"But," said Trudy earnestly, "she must hate having her class taken away from her like that. She doesn't like teaching boys."

"Who does?" laughed the other.

To her surprise, Trudy answered: "I do! I'm going to persuade Mr. Morison to give Miss Bone back her girls!"

With this determination, she went straight to the headmaster's room. She found him putting on his gown.

"Good morning, Miss Lawson. Something gone wrong?"

"Not exactly. Mr. Morison, I want to ask a favour. I like teaching boys. Can you give me 5B, please, and let Miss Bone have her girls?"

He regarded her, puzzled. "You don't know what you are asking. I was trying to make things easy for you."

"Well, I don't want things made easy. The best way to learn is to have things hard."

He laughed, but there was a glint of admiration in his eyes. "You are a very extraordinary young lady. You may have the boys, then, till the end of the week. By that time, you'll be glad to get rid of them."

Her chin went up. "Don't be too sure!"

He placed his hand on her shoulder. "Miss Bone, a tough old veteran, finds these boys difficult to handle. You are in for a bad time, but at least you've got spirit!"

He went with her to the boys' classroom where Miss Bone was already unlocking her desk, though the children were still in the playground. Sourly, she looked at Trudy while the head explained the situation.

"So we'll let Miss Lawson have a trial run with the boys, Miss Bone?"

She laughed dryly. "Certainly, if she wishes. It won't be for long!" and gathering her things, she left the room.

"A word of warning," said Mr. Morison. "Let the class see from the start that you will stand no nonsense. Their last teacher used the tawse freely. It's the only language they understand. But perhaps you don't believe in corporal punishment."

"Well," she confessed, "some cases really need it, I suppose, but they are very big boys and I don't think I could whack them hard enough. I'd better not try."

"Just send the hard cases to me," he advised.

"I hope I'll not have to. I can't believe it's true that punishment is the only language they understand."

"Ah, Miss Lawson—" he shook his head—"you are going to get some illusions shattered!"

For this Trudy was quite prepared. She knew that her short experience as a governess to two boys had not taught her everything, and her heart quaked a little as the class of forty came marching into the room, noisily at first, until they saw the headmaster. Then they calmed down and sat eyeing them both with expressions of great innocence.

Mr. Morison thereupon lectured them on courtesy to teachers and to their new mistress in particular, warning them that wrong-doers would be firmly dealt with by him. Then he left the room.

The silence which had met his words was immediately broken by whispers and shuffling. Trudy asked them to stand and say the Lord's Prayer. While they were intoning it, she prayed hard herself that she might find a way of dealing with the spirited crowd before her.

She had no fear for the Bible lesson. The dramatic story of Daniel in the lion's den was just the kind of thing to appeal to boys like this, and they listened quite willingly, though inclined to be restless. It was with the arithmetic lesson that they got out of hand.

While she was putting sums on the board, they talked and tittered behind her back, but when she confronted them, she could spot no one to blame.

Back she turned to the board, but she had just done a line of figures when a wad of wet blotting paper came past her shoulder and struck the board with a 'plop!' She stood for a moment watching it slither down and then she swiftly swept her eyes over the rows of blank faces.

"Stand up the boy who threw that paper!" she demanded.

No response.

"To do such a thing was wrong, of course," she went on, "but not to own up to it is worse. I shall give the boy thirty seconds to stand up." She studied her watch for the allotted time, amid silence. There was no movement. "Very well." It would not do to let them see she was at a loss. "The lesson will go on. I shall deal with the matter later."

Something in her tone awed them, for they settled down more quietly. But she knew the trouble was not over. Go to the headmaster? No, not already. He would only say: "I told you so."

During the afternoon break she sat in the staff room deep in thought, but no solution presented itself. Before the bell rang she went back to the room, happening to glance over the glass door before entering. At the blackboard were two boys, who ought to have been in the playground. One of them, she recalled, had sat in the front seat, seemingly obedient and well behaved. He had red hair and pale-coloured eyes and his name was Tom

MacTavish. He had a piece of chalk in his hand and was making a sketch on the board which was causing his companion great amusement.

Trudy crept away again, to think what to do. At least she knew who the culprit was, this time!

After the bell, she went into the room along with the class. A glance at the board showed her a sketch of herself with large feet and standing-up hair, entitled 'our new teacher'. She took absolutely no notice of it, or of the giggles that went on all round. She told them to open their reading books, and then, in a tone as stern as she could command, said: "Stand up, MacTavish!"

The boy shot to his feet, electrified. "Come out," she said. "Go to the board and take up the chalk."

He did so, while the class wondered.

"You are fond of drawing?" asked the new teacher.

"No, Miss—I mean, yes, Miss," he stammered.

"Well, you are going to get plenty of it. Look at that sketch, and tell me how many you could get room for on the blackboard, just the same?"

He looked. "About twenty, Miss."

"Well, go ahead and draw twenty."

The boy's face was crimson. "I don't want to, Miss."

"It's either that, or bringing Mr. Morison to see it. Which?"

"I'll do it, Miss."

Trudy went on with the reading lesson, which got great attention, except for a surreptitious glance or two at the unfortunate artist. Now and again, Trudy would stop to look, too.

"No," she would say, "you haven't got that one right! The feet are not big enough. Rub it out and do another."

By the time he was finished, she was sure MacTavish would never draw a sketch of her again. He was completely humbled, for four o'clock had come and gone and he was missing a game of football.

Trudy, alone in the room with him, said: "Well, MacTavish, you can clean them all off now. Do you think it's been worth it?"

"No, Miss," he admitted.

"And that trick you played in the morning—" by this time she had guessed he must be the culprit —"That wasn't worth it, either, was it?"

Shame-faced—"No, Miss," he mumbled. Then—"Please, will you punish me for that and get it over?"

There was something quite likeable about MacTavish. She smiled. "No, I want you to think up your own punishment. Come to me first thing in the morning and tell me what you think it ought to be."

This was something quite new; she could see she had him puzzled. All the better; it would keep him guessing.

But she felt quite tired out with her two days of teaching. Going into the staff room, she was in time to confront Miss Bone hurrying out. Surely she would be better disposed towards her now?

But no. Miss Bone stopped, looked her up and down and said: "This trying to get in with the Head by taking the boys, Miss Lawson—don't think I don't see through it!" And she walked off in high dudgeon.

There was no pleasing some people, it seemed. However, she would win her round, yet. That was what made life worth while—playing up to a challenge and winning through!

* * * * *

On Friday afternoon at four o'clock, Mr. Morison said to her: "Well, Miss Lawson, would you like to get the girls back on Monday?"

"No, thank you," she replied. "I'll keep the boys, if you don't mind. I haven't got them disciplined yet, but I'm still hoping."

"That's the stuff. But, look here, do take a rest at the week-end, you look fagged out!"

Which was only too true. Her throat was sore, her head ached and her limbs seemed made of lead. Nothing really wrong, of course; it was just the continual strain of trying to keep order. How she was looking forward to relaxing at home in sympathetic company!

Nancy was at home that evening, and to their delight, David appeared after tea to say he had the week-end off. They foregathered in Ping's room and it was quite like old times.

The room looked very bright with David's murals round the walls and all the homey things they had collected to cheer the invalid. Mrs. Lawson was seated on the easy chair doing her perpetual darning, Nancy, glad to get out of her uniform for once, sat drying her hair, while David made some trial sketches for a design. Trudy had a bundle of exer cises in front of her, but she did not feel in the mood for correction. Flat on his back, Ping lay listening to them all and occasionally putting in a word for himself.

David looked up from his drawing board.

"I saw Esther yesterday, but she didn't see me!" He sounded aggrieved.

"Really? Tell us about it," said Trudy eagerly.

"Well, I had a late lunch and was going back to work when I happened to see a 'crocodile' of schoolgirls ambling along the road. Two teachers were in front, and one of them was Esther!"

"You should have spoken to her," said Nancy.

"And given her a red face in front of them all? No fears. All the same, I wanted to." His voice was wistful.

"How did she look?" Trudy asked.

"Lovely, as usual. Very young to be a teacher. I just hope those girls are decent to her!"

"Don't worry, she'll be having a better time than Trudy. How was the Terrible MacTavish to-day?" Nancy asked.

"Subdued, but it won't last." David had to be told about the problem pupil.

"So you made him think up his own punishment?" he laughed.

She nodded. "He asked me next day if he could write, a hundred times: 'I must respect my teacher,' and I agreed. He's got his good points, you know. Very often it's a boy's home life that makes him what he is. If you could only get at the parents!"

"I'll think you were jolly brave to take on that

class," declared Nancy. "Just thinking of you makes me patient with the ward sister, when she gets on to me for something that's not my fault. Am I to blame if a patient gets his bedclothes ruffled?"

"Some people are maddening," agreed David. "There's a chap in the drawing office with me who's always doing mean things. He bears me a grudge because I've been put over his head, but it's not my fault he hadn't an art school training."

"And do you try to be patient, too?" asked his mother quietly.

"Well, it's difficult, Mum, but I do try to follow the Pattern."

She knew what he meant and was thankful that David, in his new job, still remembered the One in Whose footsteps she had taught him to follow.

Ping had not spoken for a long time. Suddenly he said: "Jesus never spoke back to his tormentors, did He? He just stood there, brave and silent. I think they must have felt very ashamed, inside themselves."

Trudy felt her eyes prickle. She had often wondered what Ping thought about during the long hours in bed. As a small boy, he had known his Bible better than any of them, and now that the activities of a boy's life were denied him, his mind was going back to the deeper things of the Scriptures.

Soon it was time for their evening hymn.

"Well, Ping, what is it to be?" asked his mother.

"That one about 'bearing shame and scoffing rude'," he replied without hesitation.

So they sang 'Man of Sorrows, wondrous Name,' and when it was finished they sang another and another, for it was so seldom now that they got the chance to be together for this sacred hour.

As Mrs. Lawson looked round her family, she had her thoughts about each one of them. Her youngest, helpless and at times so hopeless, drew the saddest thoughts of all, but he was livelier than he had been, and, please God, some day would be able to take an active part in life again. Nancy, blossoming into womanhood, impulsive and good-hearted—what lay before her in her nursing career? David, a man now, eager to get on in life and—it was no secret to a mother's eyes—on the verge of falling in love—was his future to be as bright as its promise?

Then there was Trudy, the standby that never failed her. What would she do without Trudy? The girl was going through a trying time just now, but no one encountering the world for the first time found it easy.

A mother could not help much, once her fledglings were on their own. They had to live their own lives, learn to battle for themselves. Her task, when they were young, was to put their feet in right paths, to give them a guiding faith. Then, when the test came, they would not fail.

The hymn they sang last of all, put her feelings into a few words.

> 'Lo! Such the child whose early feet
> The paths of peace have trod,
> Whose secret heart with influence sweet
> Is upward drawn to God.

Dependent on Thy bounteous breath,
We seek Thy grace alone,
In childhood, manhood, age and death,
To keep us still Thine own.'

As the hymn finished, she and Trudy exchanged glances and smiled, as if reading each other's thoughts.

CHAPTER VI

MacTAVISH VISITS PING

DAVID had not forgotten the time and place where he had seen Esther and the line of girls from St. Bride's school. Though he had no hope of her speaking to him, he contrived one day, the following week, to be on the same spot, in the hope of seeing her.

Feeling rather foolish, he waited about for ten minutes and was just moving away, when the class of girls came in sight. He walked towards them slowly, on the other side of the street. Yes, there was Esther, in the company of a tall, severe looking mistress whose glance made him long to turn and flee. But Esther was looking across. He smiled and touched his hat and saw her smile too, and hesitate. Then they all passed on, the girls looking back out of curiosity.

David kicked a stone moodily. Well, what had he expected? She had smiled at him and that ought to be enough. He turned on his heel and resigned himself to going back to work.

Then he heard light footsteps behind him and a voice calling: "David! Stop!"

There, out of breath, was Esther, her demure hat awry, her cheeks pink with exertion.

"I've escaped!" she laughed. "As soon as we got round the corner, I asked Miss Sinclair to excuse me and doubled back!"

"Good for you—" he could not keep the delight

from his voice—"I hope it won't mean trouble for you."

"Why should it, I'm not a pupil! Bit of a dragon, Miss Sinclair, she makes me feel about ten years old. But I simply had to speak to you, David!"

"And I had to speak to you, Esther!"

"Tell me about the family. I had a letter from Trudy, of course, but you have seen them, haven't you?"

He told her about the week-end. "If you had just been there it would have been perfect."

She blushed. "Thanks for that crumb of comfort. I need something to boost my morale! Tell Trudy I am the youngest teacher here, and they don't let me forget it. Worse than Trudy, I'm at their mercy all the time. No getting away at four o'clock!"

He frowned. "It's a shame. Don't put up with it!"

"I've got to. I daresay it's good for me to be kept humble. And I do love teaching, David."

"Still," he argued, "you mustn't let them make you unhappy. You're not a prisoner all the time, are you?"

"Not quite. I could go out in the evenings, I suppose. Up till now, there's been no place to go."

Then David became very bold. "Come out with me tomorrow, Esther. If it's fine we could have a walk somewhere."

Her eyes were very bright. "Really? I'd love that, David. I could meet you about here, at seven o'clock. That do?"

"Sure," he said happily.

Esther had to leave him then, to race after the class she had deserted. Meeting David had made a wonderful difference! She had felt so closed in, so friendless, and now here was a way of escape.

The severe Miss Sinclair gave her a prim look.

"Miss Moore, I must say your behaviour is no model for these girls! I suppose you went back to speak to that young man. Deplorable!"

"But his sister is my best friend, Miss Sinclair. I was enquiring for her."

"H'm! I seem to have heard that story before. If you wish to remain at St. Bride's, you will have to cut out all that sort of thing, Miss Moore."

Esther felt a wave of anger, but said nothing. During school hours, of course, she intended to abide by the rules. But her evenings were no business of Miss Sinclair's, surely?

Her hand went up to touch the little pansy brooch at her neck and her lips curved in a smile. David's brooch. The dearest thing in her possession.

* * * * *

Trudy was just leaving for school when she met the postman with a letter from Esther. She scanned it swiftly.

"What do you think, Mum, Esther and David have met! She left the school 'crocodile' to speak to him and they've made a date for tonight! I'm so glad, aren't you?"

To Mrs. Lawson the news was no surprise. "It will keep them from being lonely," she observed.

"Poor Esther, her lot is no better than mine, really. She has a 'Miss Bone' too, only hers is called Sinclair. But she says she loves her pupils and, of course, they are very intelligent. They haven't got low I.Q.'s like my lot."

"I.Q.'s?" enquired her mother.

"Intelligence Quotients. In other words, 5B is plain stupid. You wouldn't believe it, Mum, they can't even copy a sentence correctly from the board, and they are nearly fifteen, some of them! Not all their fault, poor dears. Mr. Morison says it's home circumstances in some cases. They are what dear old Becky used to call 'twisted mortals'."

"And you are trying to untwist them? It seems a big task for a young thing like you."

"The younger the better." With a farewell kiss and a 'Goodbye!' to Ping, Trudy went off to face another day of trial and tribulation.

The boy MacTavish had seemingly forgotten his humbling experience of last week and it took her all her time to maintain order, especially as he had an ally—a big, black-browed boy called Paton. Enemy number one and number two, Trudy called them. She was sure that but for this couple, the class would be easy to handle. Yet she was determined to manage them herself, rather than report them to the Head.

In the staff room, Miss Bone never looked her way, but she expected nothing else. Miss Kennedy and the others were quite pleasant. They appreciated the fight she was making, and occasionally gave her good advice.

From the beginning she could see that this was going to be a difficult day. Intelligent or not, MacTavish and Paton were clever enough to keep the class unruly without being found out. Talk, talk, chatter, chatter, even a low whistle now and again, but nothing that could be brought home to them. Then the class began to ask out for 'a drink of water', one after the other. During the history lesson Paton put up his hand:

"Please, Miss——"

"No more drinks of water, Paton!"

"But please, Miss, I'm dying of thirst!"

"You can last out till four o'clock."

"But, Miss, I'm not a camel," retorted Paton, and the class laughed, MacTavish loudest of all.

Trudy carried on with the lesson. Suddenly half a dozen hands shot up.

"Please, Miss, Paton's drinking the ink!"

There, slumped over his desk, was enemy number two, with the inkwell at his lips, and trickles of ink running down his chin.

"Stand up, Paton!" He shuffled to his feet. "Are you trying to poison yourself?"

"Please, Miss, I had to drink something!"

"Serve you right if you were made to drink ink instead of just pretending. Sit down and behave yourself!"

But she felt that the victory lay with Paton and so did the class. If she did not get the better of these two very soon, she would have to give in.

Not for the first time, Trudy took refuge behind the open lid of her desk, blew her nose, and surreptitiously dried her eyes. At the same time she conceived a plan which probably was unheard of; but at least it was worth trying.

As the boys were filing out at four o'clock, she told the two trouble makers to wait behind. There they stood before her, Paton frowning and defiant, MacTavish grinning and blinking his eyes.

"Well, boys, do you know why you are being kept in?"

McTavish shuffled and Paton growled:

"You can't punish me, I've done nothing!"

"I have no intention of punishing either of you," she said.

They looked at her unbelievingly, and their teacher continued:

"I want you to do something for me. I have a brother about your own age. But he is not so fortunate as you are. A few months ago, he rescued a boy from a cliff and was badly hurt. He is lying on his back at home, for he can't walk. Perhaps he will never walk again."

They looked at her, their expressions changing.

"He doesn't see many people, so I wondered if you would come home with me some day and talk to him."

The boys looked embarrassed; then Paton said: "If you really want us to, Miss!"

"Yes, I do. Will you come tomorrow?"

They promised, and she let them go. She had no doubt about her mother welcoming her refractory pupils. To invite them home was the sort of thing she would have done herself.

Next afternoon, Paton and MacTavish appeared in their best suits with their hair plastered down and an important look on their faces. Their behaviour was exemplary and the class was correspondingly quiet. She actually managed to teach them the geography of France.

After school, she set off homeward with the two boys. They were red-faced and self-conscious, but the warm welcome they got from Mrs. Lawson set them at ease.

"You are very tall, quite a young man," she said to Paton, who blushed at the compliment.

Then they were taken to Ping's room. They entered on tip-toe and hung back shyly, looking round at David's murals. Ping held out a thin hand and MacTavish took it in his big, rough paw.

"Please sit down where I can see you! I don't see many boys. The ones in my class used to come, but they are beginning to forget. You see, I have been in bed for a long time," the invalid explained, when he was left alone with the visitors.

"It's hard lines on you," murmured Paton. "I'd hate not to be able to walk."

"Yes, it's awful," agreed Ping. "But not so bad since I found out that my imagination has legs. And everybody is kind to me. Trudy—Miss Lawson, you call her—is terribly good, only she's always so tired nowadays."

MacTavish looked guilty. "I guess it's us that make her tired."

Ping went on: "I used to torment my teachers,

too, but if I could only go to school, I'd change all that! How do you like my brother's pictures?"

"Did your brother paint these?" MacTavish exclaimed. "My, how clever!"

"They keep me company," said Ping. "All these Bible people are real to me. I never get tired of looking at Jesus' face." He looked up at it now, in the mural where our Lord was saying: 'Suffer the children to come unto me'.

The boys sat looking at it, too, and some of the gentleness and love which David had depicted there stole into their own hearts and made them thoughtful.

"That wee girl He is holding in His arms is just like the baby next door," were Ping's next words. "Her name is Bunty, and she comes in to see me sometimes."

"Is your brother a real artist?" asked Paton.

"Oh, yes. Besides painting pictures, he designs patterns for cloth."

MacTavish said eagerly: "That's what I'd like to do!"

"Oh, yes, I remember now—you're the one that drew my sister on the blackboard, aren't you?"

MacTavish flushed. "Ach, that was the first day, before I knew her. I wouldn't do it now."

"Draw me something," said Ping. "There's a paper and pencil on that table."

MacTavish busied himself with the pencil, then handed the result to Ping. "It's a porter with a barrow. I'm best at that."

The wonderfully realistic sketch made Ping smile.

"This is good. May I keep it?" he asked.

"Sure!" The boy was flattered.

When Trudy came in to say that tea was ready—"Look what Mactavish drew!" said Ping.

"Very good, indeed. You are quite an artist, MacTavish."

"Nothing like your brother, Miss. I wish I had pictures like these at home!"

Trudy realised the probably neither of these boys had seen any real works of art.

"I'll take you to the art galleries some day," she promised.

They had a wonderful tea, to which the boys did full justice. Before they went away Trudy brought a picture from her own room.

"This is for you, MacTavish. It was my brother's and he said I was to give it to someone who would appreciate it. A great artist called Holman Hunt painted it. It's called 'The Light of the World'."

The boy gazed thoughtfully at the figure of Christ, standing alone in a dark landscape, with a lighted lantern in His hand.

"It must be Jesus," he said solemnly. "He's knocking at a door, wanting in."

"Yes, that's right. He knocks at the doors of all our hearts. Take the picture home and think about it, MacTavish. Thank you for coming to see Ping. Will you come again?"

"Yes, Miss! Thank you, Miss!" they responded eagerly.

* * * * *

There was no doubt about it, that visit made a big difference to the behaviour of the two trouble-makers. Not that they became perfect all of a sudden. They were still restless and talkative, occasionally inciting the others to mischief. But Trudy's appeals did not go in vain. She had only to speak to them in private for a few minutes, to ensure at least a spell of good conduct.

Now that discipline was improved, she was able to give her mind up to teaching them, How discouraging were the results! If facts went in at one ear, they immediately slipped out at the other. Granted, they could not help being unintelligent, but they were lazy as well. 'Patience,' she told herself, 'I must have patience!'

Relations with Miss Bone got no better. She stopped Trudy in the corridor one day to say stiffly:

"By the way, Miss Lawson, I would like to give you a piece of advice. I have heard that that boy MacTavish is boasting that he and Paton had tea at your home, and you made him a gift of a picture. Is this true?"

"Certainly, Miss Bone. There's no harm in that, surely?"

"It doesn't do," declared the other. "These two boys will take advantage."

"On the other hand, they have become much more biddable."

"And," persisted the other, "as for giving them presents! Encouraging greed. MacTavish is out for all he can get. It's a wonder he didn't lift some valuable or other."

The words made Trudy angry. "I'd rather think the best of people, not the worst, Miss Bone! MacTavish is not a vicious boy. He's only wild and badly brought up."

"Very well!" scorned the other. "Have it your own way, but take my word for it, you'll be sorry!"

CHAPTER VII

WHO IS THE CULPRIT?

IT was Saturday afternoon and Esther was free for the rest of the day. The weather was cold, for winter was on the way, and she put on her coat with the fur collar and the plain little felt hat against which her golden hair shone brightly. Her eyes had a soft light in them, for she was going to meet David at Martonbury Cross.

She had just turned the corner of a busy street, when she came face to face with a middle-aged woman with dark eyes, who smiled at her with instant recognition.

"It's Esther Moore!" she exclaimed.

"Mrs. Crawford, oh, I am pleased to see you! I was coming to visit you some day. I am teaching in St. Bride's School now."

The Crawford family ran the mission where she and Trudy used to help in their college days, when they were not too busy with studies.

Mrs. Crawford was pleased to hear of Esther's good post. "And Trudy Lawson—has she started teaching yet?"

Esther explained that Trudy was in a Drumleigh school, and told her about Ping's accident.

"Poor little fellow. It's just like Trudy to give up better things to be beside him. Now, my dear, you simply must come and see us. Can you come for tea to-day?"

Esther hesitated: "Well, the truth is, I'm meeting a friend—Trudy's brother."

Mrs. Crawford's eyes twinkled. "I see. Well, if he doesn't object, why not bring him too—say about five o'clock?"

Esther thanked her and hurried on to meet David. There he was, waiting at the corner, the best looking young man in Martonbury—or anywhere else, in her estimation.

His eyes lit up when he saw her. "I'm always so afraid they won't let you get out!" he exclaimed.

"Oh, they're not as bad as that. David, how would you like to come and have tea at the Crawfords'? We'll have time for a walk first."

He was not too pleased at first, for he grudged sharing her with anyone, but she managed to persuade him.

"The Crawfords are such hospitable folk! Next to the Lawsons, they're my favourite family," she told him.

So, after walking through the suburbs and back by a different route, they came to the Crawfords' villa. It was a homely house and although Mrs. Crawford was in alone, she was not lonely, for on the walls were dozens of photographs of her grown-up family and their children.

Soon afterwards, Mr. Crawford came in and with him Derek, the only son at home. He worked in a Martonbury bank and played for the singing at the mission meetings.

"It's good to see you again, Esther! How is Trudy?" he asked eagerly.

She gave him the news about her friend.

"She will be too busy to write poetry now, I suppose?" he queried.

"Much too busy, but the muse is bound to spring up again sooner or later!"

Derek and Trudy had a lot in common, she remembered. Probably he would have been better pleased if she and not herself had come to Martonbury!

After tea, Mr. Crawford said: "I don't suppose you two would care to come to our Saturday night meeting? There is a lantern show, with tea and buns as usual."

Esther had intended going back to correct some exercises but that seemed very dull and dutiful. She looked at David enquiringly.

"I'd love to," he said. "My digs aren't exactly inspiring."

"Nor St. Bride's School on a Saturday night," laughed Esther, so they all started to get ready for the meeting.

Looking round the hall when they arrived, she saw that nothing had changed since her student days. There was the same brightness, the same atmosphere of friendliness and good fellowship. Dene's Court was one of the few cheerful spots in the east end of the town.

In the front rows sat the children, with the parents and old folk behind, and at the back were gathered the young men and women. They had come here out of their workaday world to hear the preaching of the Gospel and to share in the simple entertainment that was provided.

How Trudy would have enjoyed being here tonight!

Listening to Derek playing the first hymn Esther was conscious of feeling very happy with David beside her like this. This dear friend of hers was of the same mind as herself concerning the deeper things of life. They both worshipped the same God and believed that only in following His Son Jesus Christ could the best things be experienced.

They enjoyed every minute of the meeting, not least the steaming hot tea brought round in kettles by smiling workers. The tea in school was always lukewarm and served without a smile. The lantern show, too—just an old-fashioned story with a happy ending—left one feeling happy and kindly disposed towards everyone.

After the last hymn had been sung and the meeting dispersed, Mr. Crawford shook hands with them.

"You will come again?"

David promised for them both. "And if you need any help, Mr. Crawford, in the way of printing bills, I could dash off some for you."

"If you ever want a soloist, I am at your service," offered Esther, "though I'm no star singer!"

They were cordially thanked and set off together along the dark street, feeling very satisfied with their evening.

"We're late tonight," said David, taking her arm. "The dragon will be prowling round looking for your blood!"

But Esther said she was not afraid of any dragon.

They stood talking for a long time at the gate of the school, unable to tear themselves away from each other.

"Oh, dear, I simply must go in!" Esther sighed. Goodnight, David!"

He let her go reluctantly. The hours with her had simply flown.

* * * * *

Esther had a key and crept quietly upstairs to her room. But she was not to get there without interruption. Going along the passage which separated the teachers' rooms from the girls' dormitories, she encountered Miss Sinclair.

"You are late, Miss Moore!"

"Not so very!" Esther tried to keep her tone light. "It's a long time till midnight yet!"

"Late enough to be loitering with a young man at the gate," retorted the other.

Esther was roused. "I don't see that is any business of yours, Miss Sinclair."

"Indeed," she gave a dry laugh, "it is the business of anyone who has young girls in charge. I could see you quite plainly from my window. Presumably they could from theirs."

"But they are in bed," she protested.

"You never know. I am warning you, Miss Moore. If you don't want trouble, you will have to mend your ways. I may find it my duty to report you. Goodnight!"

Esther went to her room, distressed and angry. Had she told Miss Sinclair she had been at a mission meeting, she would not have been believed. Some people there were who would believe only the worst. What a lot of harm they did in the world! However, she would get things off her mind by writing to Trudy and telling her everything. She would be interested to hear about Derek Crawford again.

Late as it was, she sat down at her small table and took up her pen.

* * * * *

When Trudy got Esther's letter, she made a point of answering it that same evening.

"So you have been at the Crawfords' with David. How I wish I could have been there, too! I'm glad Derek has not forgotten me. I promised to write to him, but so much has happened I keep putting off.

"I am sorry you have 'got in bad' with your Miss Sinclair. I guess you and David won't stand at the school gate again, the horrid, spying creature. My Miss Bone is just as disagreeable as ever, but my two bad boys are improving. I took them to the art galleries last week, and you should have seen the wonder on their faces! And, believe it or not, their questions were amazingly intelligent!

"I think we teachers waste a lot of time trying to cram knowledge into brains that just won't take it. What we ought to be doing is arousing interest in things that are good and fine. Make the pupils enthusiastic about something, and scrap the timetable altogether! But, alas, the authorities would have something to say, and we'd probably get our walking tickets.

"You will have heard from your father that we had him for lunch last Sunday. He is missing you, but it won't be long now till the Christmas holidays —speed the day! Ping is no better, though fairly cheerful. Nancy gets into the dumps occasionally, because of interfering sisters. Sometimes she wishes she had taken up something easier than nursing. I tell her she should be glad she's not a schoolma'am!

"But, seriously, I wouldn't be anything else, would you? Yours aye, Trudy."

* * * * *

Just before the Christmas holidays something happened in Balfour Street School which caused an unpleasant stir.

The boys in Trudy's class were among the oldest in the school and they were sometimes called on for duties outside their lessons. One morning the Head came in to ask for a responsible boy to fill the inkwells in some of the classrooms. Tom MacTavish looked so eager that she immediately suggested him for the task.

"You are sure he is trustworthy?" asked Mr. Morison.

"Yes, I am sure. MacTavish is one of my best-behaved pupils nowadays."

The boy glowed with the praise and went off happily to do the task. He came back after the forenoon break and sat down at once to do his sums.

Some minutes later there was a sharp tap at the door and Miss Bone entered, her face grim.

"I wish to speak to MacTavish, if you please!"

MacTavish stood up, obviously surprised.

"You were in my room alone filling inkwells at the break?" she demanded.

"Yes, Miss."

"Very well. You took something from my desk, MacTavish. You will please hand it over immediately!"

The boy's face crimsoned. "Please, Miss, I took nothing!"

She turned to Trudy. "Of course I did not expect him to admit it, but he has stolen my watch. I never lock my desk at the break, for I trust the girls in my class."

Trudy was in a dilemma. "I am sure MacTavish is not a thief, Miss Bone."

"You don't know him!" snapped the angry woman.

The boy was brought out to the floor and made to turn out his pockets. Nothing was revealed there but the usual odds and ends a boy collects.

"He has hidden it somewhere, of course. You had better come with me to the Head, my lad!"

Trudy had to let him go. He followed Miss Bone with a sullen, revengeful look on his face. If he had not taken the watch—and Trudy did not believe he had—this accusation was going to undo all the good she had done him.

When he returned, his face was pale and his eyes glittery. Afterwards, Trudy went to the Head herself.

"You can't pin this on to MacTavish," she pleaded. "I would know if he were telling lies, Mr. Morison."

"He has all the appearances of guilt, and had an excellent chance to steal the watch," commented the other.

"But how could he know it was in the desk?"

"He may have opened it out of curiosity. He will be suspected until the mystery is solved, I'm afraid. Miss Bone is quite sure her own class is innocent."

In the afternoon MacTavish lounged sullenly at his desk, refusing to work. Trudy left him alone. If he were being accused unjustly, he had every right to rebel, she considered.

When he left the room at four, she followed him along the corridor. He went striding along in an ugly mood and when a small boy brushed against him, he gave him a push. The boy fell heavily to the ground and immediately the headmaster, who had been watching too, came swiftly along.

"MacTavish, go to my study!"

Everyone knew that meant a beating, and Trudy waited uneasily for MacTavish to reappear. He came out at last and she could tell by his face that he had not been spared. In this mood he might be capable of anything. She laid a hand on his arm:

"Tom, please don't go home feeling like that!"

He gave her an unseeing look, pulled his arm away and shot off out of the door. Mr. Morison appeared from his room.

"Well, has he gone? The impudent fellow had

the nerve to cheek up to me. I've given him something he won't forget in a hurry!"

Trudy said sadly: "I think it was a pity to thrash him. Don't you see it was natural for him to feel angry, after being wrongly accused of stealing?"

"Natural or not," was the reply, "he had no right to bully that small boy. As for the watch—what proof is there that he didn't steal it?"

"There is no proof that he did," insisted Trudy.

He put his hand on her shoulder. "Don't fret yourself about MacTavish, Miss Lawson. He's a bad 'un. I know how to deal with him!"

Trudy wondered. She could not get MacTavish out of her mind. He had looked so unhappy, almost desperate, and she longed to do something to help him.

* * * * *

Next day the boy did not appear at school.

"That's proof if any was wanted," declared Miss Bone. "The school officer must go after him at once!"

But Trudy pleaded with Mr. Morison to let her go to MacTavish's home at the lunch hour.

"Well, it's highly irregular, but if you think you can do any good, Miss Lawson——"

Mill Street, where MacTavish lived, was a narrow thoroughfare with high tenement buildings which shut out both light and air. On this December day it looked very hopeless and drab, and she felt sorry for the children who were brought up in such surroundings. Everything seemed against them from the start.

She climbed three flights of stairs before coming to the door. The first time she rang, no one came, so she went on ringing and at last she heard footsteps. The door opened a crack and a voice said:

"What is it you want?" It was MacTavish himself.

"Tom, it's Miss Lawson. Why are you not at school?"

The door opened wider. "I've got a headache, Miss."

"That's not true. There's nothing wrong with you. MacTavish, are you a coward?"

He said vehemently: "I'm not a coward, Miss! I'm not going back to their old school. They hate me there. They call me a thief!"

"Listen," she said, "are you in alone? I'd like to talk to you."

Reluctantly, he led the way through a narrow lobby into the kitchen. It was poorly furnished and very untidy. But her heart lifted when she saw above the fireplace the picture she had given him—'The Light of the World.'

"Where is your mother, MacTavish?"

"She's out working. My Dad has been in hospital for months."

"I'm sorry. Have you any brothers or sisters?"

"Ay, Miss, four. They're all at school. My Mum thinks I'm at school, too."

"Well, Tom, I came to take you back with me. Are you coming?"

He stood there, sullenly. "Miss, I didn't steal that watch!"

She was positive he spoke the truth. "I believe you, Tom."

His face lit up. "You do, Miss? Ay, but none of the rest do. They'll take it out of me. That was an awful hammering I got, Miss!"

She smiled. There was something very frank about MacTavish. "You ought not to have pushed that little boy."

"I know, Miss. I didn't know what I was doing—I was so mad."

"I quite understand, Tom, but that's what you've got to guard against. Nobody should get so 'mad' they don't know what they're doing. Now get your books and come with me."

He stood his ground. "They'll torment me. They'll tell lies about me."

She pointed to the picture on the wall. "Tom, they tormented Him, too, and told lies about Him. He was wrongly accused of much worse things than you. Yet he bore the 'shame and scoffing rude' and would not even blame his enemies. You know what they did to Him, don't you?"

"Ay," he said, "they nailed Him to a cross."

"He knew what they intended to do, yet He would not run away. What would He think of you, afraid to go to school?"

He hung his head.

"Come, then, Tom. When they see you facing up to things, they'll think the best of you."

She managed to persuade him at last. Leaving

him in the playground, she went straight to Mr. Morison to report.

"You'll not say anything about his absence this morning?" she pleaded.

He smiled at her earnestness, and promised to let it pass. "All the same, we must get to the bottom of this watch mystery."

"It won't be my fault if it isn't solved," she promised.

"By the way, have you had any lunch?" he asked.

"Not a bite, but what does that matter?"

He shook his head. "You mustn't let your fervour run away with you. Teachers must eat. Hurry down to the lunch room, there's still time to get something!"

After she went, he became very thoughtful. What other member of his staff would forego lunch for the sake of a scallywag like MacTavish? He had been amazed at her successful handling of the wild class of boys. This young teacher certainly had the right stuff in her; would there were more like her!

CHAPTER VIII

A ROMANCE

NEXT day, though MacTavish came to school without trouble, there was still no news of Miss Bone's watch. In the afternoon, Miss Bone herself was absent, a thing which had seldom happened before. Her mother was ill and she would not be back for a few days.

Trudy's boys got gymnastics last period and she was usually free, but to-day she was asked to take over Miss Bone's class.

She had taught these girls on her first day and they were not quite strangers. She wondered, not for the first time, if the culprit might not be one of them. Miss Bone had questioned them, of course, but probably not minutely, as she was so sure of MacTavish's guilt.

Trudy made up her mind to appeal to them.

After demanding their attention, she began:

"Girls, you know your teacher is absent to-day because of illness at home. That must be a very worrying thing for her. There is something else she is worried about, too. You have already heard how her watch was taken from her desk. The person who did it has not been found."

A hand went up. "Please, Miss, it was that boy, MacTavish!"

So not only the staff but pupils thought him guilty.

"I think you are wrong, you know. Nobody saw

MacTavish take the watch, and it was not found on him. You must prove a person guilty before you can accuse him."

The girl flushed. "Everybody knows what MacTavish is!"

To that Trudy replied, sharply: "MacTavish may be wild but he is not necessarily dishonest. At the moment he is very unhappy. For one thing, his father is ill in hospital. How would you like to be in his place?"

They looked embarrassed.

"Someday," she went on, "you girls will be women, and people will turn to you for sympathy. A woman has a special part to play, you know, to be kind and loving. Think of this boy and what he is going through. Be sorry for him. Then ask yourselves—is there anything you can do to help find the real thief?"

There was absolute silence and she scrutinised each face carefully. All eyes met hers frankly except those of a dark, untidy looking girl called Sally White. Instinctively she felt that this girl knew something.

When the bell rang for dismissal she was not at all surprised to find that Sally had waited behind.

"Yes, Sally?"

"Please, Miss——" suddenly she broke down in tears. Trudy put her arm round her.

"So it was you, Sally. I am very glad you have owned up." A poor unhappy looking girl she was. Who knew what temptation had been hers?

"I've been miserable, Miss," she sobbed. "I

wanted to confess right away, but I was frightened of Miss Bone. I've got the watch in my bag. It's no good to me at all. I wouldn't dare wear it!"

From a corner of her shabby schoolbag she brought the little gold watch and laid it in Trudy's hand.

"I didn't think of anybody else getting the blame, or I wouldn't have done it, Miss. I'm sorry for MacTavish. What do you think they will do to me?"

The girl was trembling.

"You have suffered a lot already from your own conscience, haven't you, Sally? I'll tell Miss Bone that. But whatever happens, you must never do such a thing again."

"No, Miss, I've had my lesson," she declared.

"Remember what you have been taught: 'Thou shalt not steal'. Say your prayers every night, Sally. Let Jesus into you heart and ask Him to keep you from temptation. You will find it easier to be honest, then. If you are worried about anything, Sally, will you come to me?"

The girl's face broke into its first smile. "Yes, Miss, I like you. I'm not frightened of you, like some other teachers."

"You needn't be frightened of anyone, if your conscience is clear, Sally."

She watched the child go, sadly. She wondered what kind of mother she had; so much depended on training and example! She would keep a special place for Sally in her own prayers.

She went straight to Mr. Morison to report that the watch had turned up.

"So you were right about MacTavish," he said. "I'll see that he is cleared, Miss Lawson. As for this girl——"

"Don't make her punishment too hard, please!"

"We'll leave that with Miss Bone."

Trudy made up her mind to go and see Miss Bone herself without loss of time.

She found the house to be a big, gloomy villa in a depressing side street. Miss Bone herself opened the door. She looked pale and tired and her lips were a thin, straight line.

Trudy began by asking for her mother's health.

"She is no better," was the reply. "Will you come in?"

The invitation was half-hearted but Trudy accepted it and was taken into a small stuffy parlour which looked as if it had not been used for years.

"Your watch has been found, Miss Bone," and she held it out to its owner.

"So! MacTavish has owned up after all."

"But it was not MacTavish," Trudy informed her. "It was one of your own girls."

A strange woman, this! Though she was glad to get her watch back, she could not get over the fact that she had been wrong about MacTavish.

"He may be innocent about this, but he is a bad boy, all the same!" she maintained.

Trudy was annoyed. "He is trying to be good, Miss Bone, and calling him 'bad' does not help him at all."

The other sniffed. "All this talk about 'helping' is just one of your crazy notions, Miss Lawson.

We should all be able to stand on our own feet. I do!"

Trudy smiled. "Everybody is not so strong minded as you are, Miss Bone. But even you might need help some day."

"Most unlikely," she returned. "And I wouldn't ask it from you, if I did."

After a plea that she would not be too hard on the girl Sally, Trudy took her leave, expressing the hope that Miss Bone's old mother would soon be better.

"You don't get better of things when you're over ninety," was the tart response.

* * * * *

"So I am still in Miss Bone's black books," Trudy wrote to Esther next day. "How are you getting on with Miss Sinclair?"

Poor Esther was not 'getting on' at all. Until David had arrived on the scene, Miss Sinclair, though not exactly pleasant, had not interfered, but now she went out of her way to cast aspersions on her at every turn. Esther did her best to please the senior teacher, but she could not give up her friendship with David, which had become the most precious thing in her life.

Her meetings with him on Saturdays were eagerly looked forward to. She liked to look nice for him, and being tired of the prim little hat she usually wore, she bought herself a new one.

Going to meet him one day, she put on the new hat before the mirror. It was a soft, turquoise felt trimmed with a jaunty feather and it suited her to perfection. Her eyes were sparkling and her cheeks glowing as she came downstairs. There at the bottom was Miss Sinclair and that nice little French mistress, Miss Lamour.

The little woman's eyes twinkled. "Ah, Mees Moore, you look exceedingly *belle* to-day! It is the new *chapeau*, is it not?"

"Yes," laughed Esther, "it is a new hat. You like it?"

"Ah, *oui*, it is *charmant*."

But Miss Sinclair eyed the new hat coldly.

"All set to make a conquest, I see," was the dry comment.

"*Mais, non*," put in the French lady, "*Ma'm'selle* is too young, is she not, to think of such things?"

"Not at all," clipped the other. "Miss Moore thinks of nothing else. Gallivanting till all hours."

Miss Lamour's eyebrows went up. "Is zat so? I would not have thought—How one can be mistaken!"

Esther was furious. "Miss Sinclair is wrong about me," she declared as she passed them and made for the door.

David was waiting at the corner and saw the mortification on her face. He took her hands in his.

"Esther, something is wrong. Tell me!"

"It's nothing," she replied. "Just Miss Sinclair again."

As they walked on, arm in arm, David's mind was troubled. He could not bear to think of Esther unhappy.

"Tell me what she said," he insisted.

With heightened colour, she repeated the taunts which had so stung her. "I didn't tell you before, David, but the other Saturday she saw us at the gate—she was spying, of course—and she threatened to report me."

David clenched his fists. "If I could get at her!"

She laughed. "You wouldn't fight her, surely!"

"No, but I'd tell her what I thought of interfering busybodies. A girl like you should not be at the mercy of a jealous old tabby like that."

She tried to calm him down. "I'll live through it, David. It won't be for ever."

"No." He clasped her arm tightly. "It won't be for much longer, if I can help it!"

There was a warmth in his voice which quickened her heartbeat. "How can you help it, David?"

"By taking you away from it all. You must know, Esther, what my feelings are. Ever since that first day Trudy brought you to tea years ago, you have been the only girl for me."

He pressed the fingers lying on his arm, wishing that they could have been alone where there were no passers-by to see them. He had not meant to say all this to-day, but she was so dear to him, and he was so grieved for her, that it all came out.

After a few seconds silence, she replied, very gently, "And you, David, have always been the only one for me."

David felt a great surge of happiness. What a difference a girl like Esther made to a man's life! 'A perfect woman, nobly planned, to warn, to comfort, and command'. He asked no more than to make a home for her and work hard for her all the days of his life.

"Esther," he went on triumphantly, "this is a great day, isn't it? Do you think you can carry on a little longer till we are ready to get married?"

Her eyes shone. "As long as you like, David. I'll be so happy waiting, Miss Sinclair can do her worst!"

As they walked on, the familiar streets and houses, all the familiar things, seemed to have acquired a wonderful glow, the reflection of their happy hearts.

"Shall we tell the others?" David asked after a while.

Esther pondered. "Wait till Christmas. Then I'd like to tell Trudy, at least. How thrilled she will be!"

"We could get engaged at Christmas," suggested David. "That is, if your father gives his consent."

"But of course he will! Any man would be proud to have you for a son-in-law, David."

But David was not so sure. Andrew Moore was a wealthy man and David's income and prospects might not appeal to him. But surely the fact that they were so much in love would weigh with him?

Though Esther deserved the best that money could buy, she also deserved what was more important—a whole-hearted love and devotion, and David could give her that without stint.

CHAPTER IX

CHRISTMAS HOLIDAYS

BALFOUR STREET School broke up the day before Christmas. Now Trudy could look forward to ten days of freedom, and a longer lie in bed each morning. No dashing out into the dark, wintry streets, no restless class to bring to order, no lessons to prepare or exercises to correct. Above all, no Miss Bone. Yes, teaching was worthwhile, but it was a hard grind that tired you out, mentally and physically.

Their one aim this Christmas was to make it a happy time for Ping, so they prepared for the day by decorating his room with holly and mistletoe, and a small, illuminated tree in the window.

On Christmas morning, Trudy peeped in to greet him. "Happy Christmas, Ping!"

He was lying awake, very thoughtful. "Will I still be lying like this next Christmas, I wonder?"

Trudy felt a rush of compassion. "Poor old Ping! But next Christmas is a whole year away. Plenty of time to get better. Look, here's a card for you. Let's see who it's from."

The card was hand-painted and showed a picture of the three wise men offering gifts to the infant Jesus. Underneath was a verse from a Christmas hymn:

'Love came down at Christmas,
Love all lovely, Love Divine;
Love was born at Christmas,
Stars and angels gave the Sign.'

Trudy looked at the signature. "It's from Brian Clyde! He has painted it himself."

Ping was thrilled. "To think a man like that would paint a picture for me! Oh, Trudy, I do wish we could see Brian and Olivia again!"

Brian was Ping's hero. He was a hero to all of them. In summer, he spent weeks painting in his studio on Barone Island, where the Lawsons had once spent a holiday in a house called "Ardensheel". In winter, he and his wife, Olivia, who was a very fine singer, toured the country in a caravan, preaching the word of God in various towns. On one memorable occasion they had come to Drumleigh. It used to be Ping's ambition to ride in that caravan with them, but now that seemed further away than ever.

Trudy knew what he was thinking, but fortunately distraction came with the appearance of the rest of the family with presents, with Rusty an excited spectator, trying as usual to leap up on the bed beside Ping, and being very crestfallen when he was removed.

Nancy had just paid a flying visit, for this was a busy day in hospital. She presented Ping with a mirror which was hung so as he could see what was going on outside the window—the bird tray and the birds feeding and people going out and in the back door.

"And in spring you'll be able to see the flowers in the rockery," added Nancy. "But by that time, you'll probably be out there yourself." Which was only echoing the hope in all their hearts.

Trudy had pasted into a book snapshots and pictures of all the places Ping had ever seen, or would like to go to—"To help your imagination take you there," she explained—"And look, here's a picture gallery of the whole family, right from the time we wore long robes. If you want to see one of us and have a laugh, just open up and there you are!"

Mum had been busy, too, making a patchwork quilt with scraps of bright material. David had helped by bringing from the factory lots of pictorial designs to make the quilt gay and colourful.

"I couldn't ever get bored with a quilt like that to study," Ping commented. "Thank you, Mum. Thank you, everybody!"

But David had not produced his present yet. Without saying a word to anyone, he had worked away at a project for weeks. Now he opened up a parcel and produced from it a wonderful array of handmade glove puppets.

There was a comical red-nosed policeman, an old, witchlike woman, a king in royal robes and his daughter, a beautiful princess with golden hair. To match her was a handsome prince, of course, but there was a villain too, very sinister looking, with a black moustache.

Ping's hands were about the only bit of him he could move freely and he immediately began to work the puppets, putting them through laughable antics and making them talk.

"David, you're a genius," complimented Trudy, "not only to make them but to think up the idea."

"I just happened to remember that long ago when

Ping had mumps, puppets were the only things that cheered him up."

"I called them 'hitjacks' when I was wee," Ping recalled, and proceeded to give names to his puppet family. 'Bobs' was the policeman and 'Grannie Mutch' the old woman, and the princess of course was called 'Goldilocks'.

"She's lovely, just like Esther," Ping remarked.

David was seen to blush. Then the door bell rang and it was Esther herself. Trudy took her upstairs for exchange of confidences. She had never seen her friend so radiant.

"How lovely to see you again, True!" She span her round the room in an access of high spirits.

"Please, leave me some breath, Esther! I'll need it to tell you everything. Who's to begin?"

"You," replied Esther. "Tell me about Miss Bone and the Terrible MacTavish."

"MacTavish isn't terrible any more. Mind you, Miss Bone keeps on warning me that he is sure to break out again, but I think we understand each other now. I used to call him enemy number one, and try to get the better of him, till I found out that it was easier to make a friend of him."

"If everybody would just do that with enemies!" exclaimed Esther. "Think of it, Trudy, there would be no more wars. Everybody would trust each other."

"Exactly what I think. If they allowed us school-ma'ams to run the world, there would soon be an improvement!"

"Sure. But I must say I'm happy enough as I am."

"Tell me about the Crawfords," urged Trudy.

"We go there every Saturday, practically. David prints bills for the mission, and I sang a solo one night. But did Derek not tell you? He said he was going to write you."

"Yes, I did get a letter," admitted Trudy.

"Derek has a soft spot for you, my girl, always asking for you. Haven't you answered his letter?"

"Well, no," she confessed. "I like Derek but I don't want to get too friendly with anyone just now. I've got my teaching to think about, and poor Ping. There's no time, really, for anything else."

"You ought to think of yourself sometimes," Esther admonished. "You make me feel so selfish."

"My dear Esther, I never met a less selfish person. It's not as if you have been having too good a time. That Miss Sinclair—how can you bear her?"

Esther actually laughed. "She makes no impact on me now. She has simply ceased to matter, I'm so happy!"

Seeing the radiance on her face, Trudy immediately guessed her secret.

"Esther, you don't mean—It can't be that you and David—?"

Esther nodded, not able to speak, and a warm, impulsive kiss passed between them.

"You are the first to know, Trudy. David is speaking to Dad tomorrow. Until then, you'll not tell anyone, will you?"

"Of course not, though I'm sure they will guess. It's bursting out of you, Esther, and David's the same. This is one of my dreams come true. Think of it—we'll be sisters!"

"You're really glad, Trudy? Some girls wouldn't be. In a way, I'm stealing David from you, and he is stealing me!"

"I don't call it stealing," maintained Trudy. "I'll love you all the more, and David too. It's a compliment to me that he should choose my best friend. Will you really be getting engaged?"

"If Dad agrees. Do you think your mother will be pleased?"

"I'm sure she will. Mum loves you like a daughter."

"And I love her too," said Esther sincerely.

Her father arrived in time for lunch, for they had both been invited to spend the day. Mr. Moore was much thinner and bore a look of strain. However, he was quite cheerful during the meal and happy to have Esther back beside him.

It was a bumper Christmas banquet with turkey and plum pudding, of which Ping got his due share. Then while Trudy and Esther washed up, their elders were persuaded to rest while David set up a puppet booth in Ping's room to give them a show with the new puppets.

When it was ready, the audience was invited to enter. New guests had arrived; the Drysdales from next door and the Lawsons' Aunt Susan, who always turned up at Christmas even though they hardly saw her during the year. Never had there been so many people in Ping's room at one time, and still more were to arrive.

They came quite unexpectedly—the Terrible MacTavish and his friend Paton. Trudy opened the door to them. They had taken great pains brushing their hair and a broad grin adorned each face.

"Please, Miss, a Happy Christmas," they said simultaneously.

Trudy shook hands with them. "How nice of you! You are just in time to see the puppet show."

She took them in, fetched two more chairs, and introduced them to the company.

David had disappeared behind the puppet booth, switching on the electric bulb which lit the platform, and the puppets came on to introduce themselves one by one.

After that, they acted a little story which David had made up, all about a beautiful princess in the clutches of a wicked villain. It ended happily, of course, with the handsome prince rescuing his lady and claiming her as his bride.

It brought forth hearty applause, and MacTavish clapped louder than any of them.

"But Miss, it's wonderful!" Then, when David appeared—"Did you really do that all yourself?"

David showed him how to work the puppets and MacTavish picked up the idea far more quickly than he did his school lessons!

"In some schools the pupils learn puppetry, you know," David told him.

"I wish they did in ours!"

"You should ask the headmaster."

"He wouldn't let us, would he, Miss?" asked Paton.

"Probably not." But the idea took firm root in Trudy's mind.

Then MacTavish suddenly remembered what he had come for.

"Please, Miss, we've got a present for Ping. Can we give it to him?"

"Please!" urged Ping.

MacTavish hastened to disclose their gift. "It's not very much," he apologised. "We had to save up for it. It's to put on the wall—see? It tells you what the weather's going to be. We thought Ping would like to know, then he could tell Miss Lawson when to take her umbrella to school."

It turned out to be a small wooden cottage with a red roof. At the door stood a little man with a big umbrella.

"It looks as if it's going to rain soon," explained MacTavish. "When it's dry, a wee lady comes out. Do you like it, Ping?" he asked anxiously.

Ping was quite fascinated, and it was put up on the wall beside him so as he could watch the movements of the cottage dwellers.

After the young folk had played at a few guessing games, Ping was seen to weary, and the guests took their leave after tea. Mr. Moore had his car and offered to run the boys home, so their day ended with a thrill. At the door Trudy heard David say to Esther's father—

"If you are at home tomorrow, Mr. Moore, may I come and see you?"

The older man hesitated. "Is it important, David?"

"Very important, sir."

"Very well," was the reply. "Make it three o'clock in the afternoon."

* * * * *

David spent the next forenoon touching up the murals in Ping's room and entertaining him with the puppets, but his mind was not on what he was doing. Trudy knew what was worrying him and she guessed that her mother did, too. After lunch he dressed himself with great care and with a grim do-or-die expression set off for the Moore's house.

It was a fine modern building, much grander than the Lawson's semi-detached villa. The grounds were well cared for by a resident gardener and everywhere there was evidence of wealth. Never would he be able to afford such splendour for Esther. With a housekeeper and a staff of servants she could know nothing of housekeeping and making ends meet. Yet when she married him, they might have to start without any servants at all. Was it fair to Esther? He was beginning to have doubts.

"Mr. Moore is expecting me," he told the trim maid who opened the door. She took him into the luxuriously furnished lounge and in a moment Esther joined him there. She was dressed in an afternoon frock of rose coloured velvet and round her neck was a string of pearls that must have cost a fortune. David's heart sank.

"David, why so glum?"

"It's just that you look so grand," he jerked out.

She put her cool hand in his. "You are not to think of me like that. I am just—your Esther."

"'My Esther,'" he repeated proudly, encircling her with his arm and kissing her soft lips. Then suddenly the door opened and Mr. Moore came in. His glance took in everything, and Esther's colour heightened.

"I'll go and leave you with David, Dad. Please be nice to him!"

Then they were alone. David took a deep breath and said the words he had rehearsed so often.

"I think you know what I came for, Mr. Moore. Esther and I are in love with each other. We want to get married some day. Will you consent to our engagement?"

He waited, eyeing the other nervously, so much depended on his reply. Mr. Moore did not meet his gaze. He sat drumming with his fingers on the arm of his chair, two lines furrowing his forehead.

"David," he began, "I like you and I like your family. You are a fine young man and I believe you will do quite well in life. But I love my daughter too much to give her to the first one who asks. She is only twenty-one and you are not much older. You are both too young to tie yourselves up."

Bitter disappointment flowed through him. "But Mr. Moore, we have known each other a long time and there has never been anyone else for either of us."

"Esther has not had a chance yet to meet many young men," said the other. Let her wait for a few years. It would not be fair to bind her just now."

"I understand," said David miserably. "I know

I cannot offer her what many another man could."

"You are right. Being fond of you, she may think just now that doing without things would not matter. But it would soon lose its novelty."

"Not if she truly loved me," David maintained.

"Oh, I believe she is in love with you, but if this is just young love—the kind that does not last—how unhappy she would be!"

There was a silence. "I could not bear to think of her unhappy," David murmured.

"Then, do not risk it. Let her be free, whether she wants it or not, to get to know other men. After a few years, if you are both still in love, it will be a different matter."

'A few years'. He might as well have said a few centuries to the impatient lover!

David rose. "Is this your last word, Mr. Moore?"

"Absolutely. I think I know what is best for my daughter. You will take my advice, I hope."

"I have no choice," David was saying when the door opened and Esther came in, sparkling and expectant.

"Well, you two, is it all fixed up?" Then she saw their faces. "Why, what's the matter? Dad, it can't be that you don't approve of David?"

"I do approve of David," said her father shortly, "but not for you. At least, not yet. He will tell you himself. I shall leave you together," and he went out of the room.

"David!" Esther clung to his arm, scanning his face with pleading eyes. "What has Dad got against you?"

"Just that I'm not old enough, nor well enough off."

"I see. Dad is still inclined to measure up people by what they possess, but you know I don't care about that, don't you?"

"Yes," he replied, "I know that, Esther. But it's true enough that I could not give you the comforts you are used to. A girl in your position could easily marry a much richer man than I am."

She laughed, rubbing her cheek against his sleeve.

"But I don't want a rich man, I want you! I shall tell Dad so."

He sighed. "Your father has made up his mind, Esther, and he is not the kind of man to change it."

This Esther well knew. "You're right, but if he sees we are determined, David—"

He shook his head. "Esther, we'll have to do what he says, and wait. In a few years we'll be older and I shall be better off—I hope! Going against him just now would create such bad feeling."

"But David!" It was a cry of distress. "I don't want to wait! I want to be engaged to you now!"

Her words put him in a dilemma. "My dear, that is what I want too, but it would not be fair to you. You might meet someone in the next year or two who would—who would suit you better. We'll keep friendly, of course, but we'll have to postpone our engagement."

Esther was near to tears. "I don't believe you want to marry me at all!" she cried, unthinkingly.

David went very pale. "That's not true, Esther, and you know it."

She was instantly sorry. "I should not have said that, David. We mustn't quarrel, whatever we do. I trust you, dear, I'll do what you think best."

He kissed her tenderly. "Though to the world we'll just be friends, our own hearts will know differently. I vow to be true to you, Esther, whatever the future brings."

She placed her hand in his. "And I vow, David, that I will be true to you, for years and years if need be."

Their eyes met and held, speaking more eloquently than words. Had Andrew Moore seen them then, he surely would have realised that all his protests would never separate those two young and loving hearts.

CHAPTER X

TRUDY'S NEW IDEA

TRUDY was in Ping's room when she heard David come in and go straight upstairs. She was puzzled. Why had he not brought Esther back with him to proclaim their engagement to the family? The first doubt assailed her. Surely Mr. Moore had not put anything in the way?

When David appeared at tea-time, pale-faced and silent, she felt certain things had gone wrong. Her mother guessed too and was very gentle with him, making no allusion to Esther. But Nancy had no such compunctions. Free for the evening, she came in as they were finishing the meal, and looked round in surprise.

"Hello, no Esther? Didn't you expect her, Trudy? I'm sure David did!"

No one spoke, but David's face flushed over.

"You do look self-conscious, David," Nancy laughed. "The minute anybody says 'Esther' you turn like a beetroot."

Without a word David rose and strode from the room.

Nancy gaped. "What have I done now?"

"Just put your foot in it as usual," Trudy told her. "Keep this to yourself, but I suspect Mr. Moore has turned down David as a future son-in-law."

"But he couldn't," protested her sister. "He ought to be proud! Oh, I know David and I wrangle a lot, but I recognise his good points. I'd like to have a word with Mr. Moore!"

"He'd silence you with a look," returned Trudy, "and that's saying something. Oh, dear, if we only knew!"

Later she went up to David's room and knocked at the door.

"Come in," said a non-committal voice. "Oh, it's you, Trudy, good! You might as well know now that there is to be no engagement—not yet awhile. But we're not giving each other up!"

He explained Mr. Moore's objections. She agreed that with any other couple they might hold good, but David and Esther were different.

"If only he could understand that there will never be anyone else for either of you!" she sighed.

"Time will prove that, if nothing else does," said David.

"Esther must be shattered."

"She's very unhappy about it, Trudy. A talk with you would do her good."

"I'll go round and see her immediately," she decided.

Esther had been crying. There were shadows under her eyes and her face was pale. In her own comfortable room with its cushioned settee and lovely modern furniture, she poured out her heart.

"I've pled with Dad, Trudy, but it's no use. He must be firm for my sake, he says; he is older and knows best. As if I don't know my own heart! I'd marry David this very minute if he'd have me! But that's the trouble—he won't go against Dad."

"I see David's point of view," declared Trudy. "The time will come when you'll be a wealthy woman, Esther. Some people might call him a fortune hunter."

Esther almost laughed. "No-one who knows him would think that of him! I suppose I oughtn't to make myself miserable, Trudy. David loves me and that is the main thing. I must cling to that." She dried her tears and attempted a smile. In time, when she got more resigned, she would learn to hide her disappointment and longing. But Trudy was grieved for her, though never doubting there would be a happy outcome.

* * * * *

School took up again after the New Year. Esther went back to Martonbury and Trudy to Balfour Street. On her first day she noticed that Miss Bone wore deep mourning and was told by Miss Kennedy that her mother had died during the holidays.

Though she had no reason to love the soured and elderly school teacher, she realised it must have been a very trying Christmas for her, and stopped her in the corridor to hold out a hand of sympathy.

"I was sorry to hear about your loss, Miss Bone."

The wrinkled face flushed and a limp hand touched hers for a moment. "Thank you, Miss Lawson."

"Is there anything I can do for you?"

"Thank you, no," she said stiffly.

"Perhaps an older person . . .? My mother would be very pleased to see you any time. We stay in Lester Avenue."

"I never pay visits," she said firmly and turned away.

What could you do with a woman like that? Trudy always had a guilty feeling when Miss Bone was near; she eyed her so accusingly—and why? Because in spite of her youth and inexperience she had managed to curb a class of boys that had been too much for Miss Bone herself. Probably it would have pleased her better had Trudy been a failure all round.

Miss Kennedy and the others noticed how she was worrying about the older teacher's attitude.

"I don't see why you can't forget about her and be happy!"

But Trudy was so made that she could not be blind to other people's troubles. She realised that Miss Bone's unpleasantness was the result of a mind not at peace with itself. Some people were unhappy through no fault of their own, like poor Esther at the moment, and darling Ping. But others seemed to shut themselves out deliberately from the best life had to offer. It was sometimes due to a twist in their natures and this, she was sure, was what was wrong with Miss Bone.

She recalled other people she had known—like old Mrs. Somers at Ardensheel—their own worst enemies. And she had seen more than one of them changed as if by a miracle, when they had given their hearts and lives over to a higher power than their own.

She was sure that Miss Bone could find happiness in this way too, become a person whom people would want to know instead of to shun. If only she and her mother could get in touch! What Miss Bone would not take from Trudy, she might be prepared to listen to from an experienced woman like Mrs. Lawson. In the meantime, however, there seemed no hope.

* * * * *

With the new term, her boys proved fairly amenable, but she felt they were finding school work a dull grind for which they had little heart.

Many of them would soon be leaving school, and they would be glad to go. Trudy thought that a shame. Your schooldays ought to be the happiest days of your life. Couldn't she do something to liven up the timetable and give some happy days to the boys who were going out into an unsympathetic word?

Suddenly she remembered about David's puppets and how he had said that in some schools puppetry was a timetable subject. She also remembered MacTavish's bright eyes and his interest in the puppet show. She wrote at once to David for information and on receiving his reply, paid a visit to Mr. Morison in his room.

"Well, Miss Lawson, what can I do for you? I hope those boys have not been troublesome?"

"No, Mr. Morison, it is not that. I'd like to speak to you, if you don't mind, about introducing puppetry into the timetable. You see, my class have several hours of art in the week. They get bored with drawing boxes and bottles, and I don't blame them, do you? Now, my brother——" and out it all came.

His face was a queer mixture of interest and disbelief.

"My dear Miss Lawson, what good do you think this new subject would do your pupils?"

"Ever so much. First they would have to make the puppets. That would give the artistic ones a chance. Then they would compose little sketches for them to act, perhaps from history. Originality and English composition come into that. Some would build the booth and that would give them practice in carpentry. As for manipulating the puppets—you can see how that would train both hand and eye."

"You seem to have thought it well out," he said, smiling.

"Of course I have, but that's not all. They would have to make the puppets speak. You get voice production there and correct pronunciation. The whole process gives a means of self-expression, and that's what those boys need."

He became very thoughtful. "I believe you have got something there, Miss Lawson. Boys must express themselves. They have to break out somehow,. and too often it is in the wrong direction. Puppets . . . well, well."

"You will see what you can do?" she asked eagerly.

"I'll think about it. No rash promises!"

But she felt quite hopeful.

Not without reason, either, for the next week he came to her to say that as an experiment, she might try out some puppetry with her class. If successful, it might be introduced into other classes too.

Trudy started off by bringing along Ping's puppets and showing how they worked. The boys were most enthusiastic and eager to start making their own as soon as possible.

David had explained the whole process to her. The best material for making the heads of the puppets was paper-mache. To make this itself was an intricate process. Newspapers had to be torn up into tiny shreds which were mixed together with water and paste and painter's 'size'.

What a day that was when the class made paper-mache! The stuff stuck to everything it touched, and the boys went home with pieces of it clinging to their clothes and their hair. When they had learned to make it properly, they went on to the next stage. For each puppet's head a cardboard tube was required, which was fixed on to the neck of a bottle. Now a ball of paper-mache was moulded on to the tube and made into the shape of a head and face.

The boys who were clever with their fingers made quite creditable faces—some comic, some tragic. The best ones were chosen to be fired in the school oven until they were hard and unbreakable. Then they were painted. If the puppet needed hair, bits of old fur were used, with strands of embroidery silk for the girl puppets.

Dressing the puppets was fun, too. All sorts of scraps were produced from their mother's rag bags. Then scissors got busy and needles were threaded and rethreaded as clumsy fingers learned to sew.

Meanwhile, the imaginative boys were making up stories and the practical ones building a booth. All was being got ready for the great day when they would begin to rehearse the puppets for a show at the end of the term.

As time went on, more teachers became interested in Trudy's venture and the other classes were frankly jealous of 5B. The boys began to feel important and even took an interest in their other lessons. School was not such a bad place after all! It was very sporting of Miss Lawson to teach them puppetry; she was really more of a friend than a teacher. They would stick in at their lessons—even the ones they didn't like—and show her!

* * * * *

Meanwhile, at home poor Ping was dreading the day when he would have to go to Nancy's hospital to have his plaster removed and get treatment for his injured back.

To leave his own cosy bed for a narrow hospital one—which he would have to keep so tidy!—and to lose sight of David's murals and all the possessions which had passed the time so pleasantly was not the worst of it. Nurses were kind, but they were not his mother. There would be no Rusty to run out and in and put pleading paws up on the bed, no familiar home sounds of doorbell ringing and meals being got ready, no cosy evening chats and hymn singing.

"I suppose I've got to go?" he observed mournfully.

"Absolutely necessary," replied Trudy. "It's the only way to get well again, Ping. It might not be for long, you know. The massage and exercises might make you fit in no time."

"And they might not," he sighed. "Nobody knows, I suppose. Anyhow, Nancy won't be far away. Do you think she might be allowed to nurse me?"

"Well, she's only a probationer, but she might be allowed to wash your face and give you your food. She will tell you all about us at home, and will tell us all about you. And, of course, we'll be in to visit you—every day if we're allowed."

The day came, as dreaded days do, and the ambulance arrived to take him away. It was Saturday and Trudy was at home.

"Son," said his mother in farewell, "though we won't be there beside you, we will be praying for you. Pray too, Ping. Remember that prayer can heal the sick and help the lame to walk. Remember Stephen Drysdale and how sight came back to him. Remember Olivia Clyde and how she found her voice again. You believed in miracles when you were a small boy, didn't you? Believe in them now, Ping, for they do happen!"

Ping's sober face broke into a smile. "I needed that little lecture, Mum. I'll not forget to say my prayers and I'll thank God for my blessings. I've got so many blessings, and you and Trudy are two of them."

The ambulance men put him skilfully on to a stretcher and bore him out. Mrs. Lawson went with him to see him settled in hospital. In the case she carried with his things was the puppet he loved best, the princess Goldilocks. Rusty ran down the path barking and Trudy had to call him back. She patted the smooth head and through tears looked down into the faithful brown eyes.

"He's gone, Rusty, old boy, but he'll come back again, never fear!" Then, waving to the departing ambulance, she returned to put Ping's room to rights. The ruffled bed, still warm, the book he had been reading, his breakfast tray with the toast half eaten—all spoke eloquently of his presence.

"Oh, Ping, how we will miss you and how lonely you will feel!" In her distress, she looked round at the murals, and saw the face that David had depicted so lovingly, smiling down at her with infinite comfort in His gaze.

"He knows," she murmured. "He knows what we are feeling just now, and tells us to be 'of good cheer'." It would not help Ping if she were mournful. The empty room must be kept bright and welcoming for his return; she would start right now and give it a thorough clean. There was nothing like hard work to make one forget.

CHAPTER XI

A TEST FOR DAVID

DURING forenoon break one day, Trudy had a visit from the headmaster.

"About this puppetry," he began, "You find the idea working all right?"

"More than all right, Mr. Morison. The boys simply love it. Some of them are even sorry they are leaving school!"

"Really? I must admit that class of yours is less of a nuisance all round. I wonder if it would work with the girls at the same stage?"

"You mean Miss Bone's class? I'm sure it would!"

"As a matter of fact," he went on, "I have had a deputation from them, asking if they couldn't have puppets too. I spoke to Miss Bone, but she says she doesn't know the first thing about them."

Trudy smiled. "I guess she said it in no uncertain terms!"

"You're right. I think you should have a talk with her. You could give her some tuition."

He was very hopeful.

"I'll certainly discuss it with her," was the doubtful reply.

"Thank you, Miss Lawson. While I am here, there is something else I'd like to mention. Miss Bone tells me that, being next door, she sometimes notices that you don't keep strictly to the timetable."

Trudy flushed. "In what way, Mr. Morison?"

"Well, Miss Lawson, in the forenoons, when you ought to be getting on with arithmetic, you are still at the Bible lesson. I thought it my duty to mention this. You young teachers must be kept on the rails. A timetable is meant to be followed, you know." It was said quite kindly.

"I do follow it," she maintained, "but occasionally I get absorbed in the Bible lesson and forget the time. It's so important for these boys leaving school that they should know their Bibles. Don't you think so, Mr. Morison?"

He said brusquely, "They must know how to count, too!"

"Of course, but most of them are as good at that as they could ever be. I'd rather see them go into the world knowing how to behave well, with the love of God in their hearts."

His brows wrinkled. "Very important, no doubt. But that is not our job. They have parents. They have Sunday Schools."

"Yes—" Trudy was determined to speak her mind, "but few of them go to Sunday School, and what do their parents teach them about good and bad? You know as well as I do, Mr. Morison, that these boys come from lax homes and have practically no training in the things that count!"

He could not contradict her. "You are young to talk like this. What do you know about it?" he asked.

"When I was at college in Martonbury," she told him, "a friend and I helped with mission work and went into many of the poorer homes. I guess the ones in Drumleigh aren't much different."

"I see. What a serious-minded young lady you are!"

"Not always," she informed him. "But there's one thing I'd like to see started in this school, Mr. Morison, and that's a weekly service, with all the school gathered together to sing hymns and listen to a short address."

"Indeed!" he observed. "Let me tell you, Miss Lawson, there is absolutely no time for that. Every minute on every timetable is taken up with something else."

"Something else that doesn't matter half so much!" she declared.

"You have half-an-hour every day for religious instruction. Isn't that enough?"

"Not nearly enough. They are just beginning to get interested when they have to stop."

He shook his head at her. "Come down to earth, Miss Lawson. Accept things as they are."

"No," she retorted, "not till I'm about eighty, and perhaps not even then."

"You've got some hard times in front of you, then."

"I know," said Trudy. "It's all I ask for; I don't want to be 'carried to the skies on flowery beds of ease'."

He laughed at that. "You are quite a crusader."

"That's what I want to be—a 'crusader'. I think that word has a lovely sound!"

Then the bell rang and Mr. Morison had to go. But she remembered what he had said about speaking to Miss Bone, and at four o'clock, she ran after the prim little teacher as she left the school.

"Mr. Morison tells me your girls are interested in puppetry, Miss Bone."

The thin lips tightened. "Anything to waste time!" she remarked.

"But it isn't a waste of time," and she argued as she had done before, describing all the advantages. "My boys are taking much more interest in school, now."

The other sniffed. "New-fangled notions don't go down with me, Miss Lawson. When I was a young teacher, I took the advice of my elders and didn't try to disrupt a whole school!"

She walked on quickly, but Trudy kept pace with her.

"Oh come, Miss Bone, you can't say that about me. If there were no new things there would be no progress."

"We can do without your kind of progress!" was the reply.

Trudy was tempted to give up, but made one last attempt.

"If you do decide to start on puppets, I'll be very pleased to tell you all I know," she offered.

Worse and worse. Miss Bone was furious.

"You would teach me my job would you! Generous, I must say, but if I ever need advice I'll not ask it from you!" and she turned the corner into the road where she lived, without a word of goodbye.

* * * * *

Next day was Saturday. To the surprise of Trudy and her mother, David walked in at tea-time without any warning. He looked thinner than at Christmas time and quite a lot older.

"How jolly, David! Are you home for the week-end?" Trudy greeted him.

He nodded. "Hope you can get me up early enough on Monday! How is Ping?"

"He has got his plaster off, but isn't walking yet or anything like it."

"Progress will be slow even at the best," commented Mrs. Lawson. "He won't be home for some time."

"Have you seen Esther lately?" Trudy dared to ask.

"Well, we don't see so much of each other now, but it's something to do with her that brought me home. I want to discuss it with you two."

Something important, they knew by his tone.

"I've had a letter from Mr. Moore, Mum. Esther has been pleading with him on my behalf."

"Good for Esther!" exclaimed his sister.

"I'd rather she hadn't, though she did it for the best. Now her father has relented—in a way."

"In what way?" asked his mother.

"He says that if I give up my present job, he will take me into his business and put me in the way of making a lot of money."

His news was greeted with silence.

"Well," he demanded, "why aren't you saying something? Don't you think it would be a good thing? We could get engaged right off, he says, and be married quite soon. Think of it!" But they were still too taken aback to reply.

"Mum, you must say something. I was depending on you!"

His mother gave him a steady look from her calm eyes.

"You are making a fairly good salary as you are, David, and you are working at something you love. You aren't suited for a business like Mr. Moore's."

"But Mum, you never get rich in jobs like mine. Enough to live on, yes, but the thousands don't roll in!"

A little smile twitched his mother's lips. "Would those thousands bring you happiness if you gave up your art, David, the one ambition you ever had?"

He looked at her with haggard eyes. "They would bring me Esther!"

"And would she be happy, knowing what you had given up for her? David, she isn't that kind of girl."

David put his face in his hands and something like a groan escaped him.

"We have all been so proud of you, David, sticking to your career through thick and thin. All our aims have been to help you get through art school, and achieve your ambition. You remember what Trudy gave up so that you could go on with your studies?"

He looked up. "Yes, I forgot about that. I'd be letting you all down, not just myself. Oh, Mum, it's so difficult to make a choice!"

She knew that. David's temptation was a strong one. It was not that he desired wealth for wealth's sake, but it seemed the only way of making sure of the girl he loved.

"Pray about it, David," advised his mother. "Tonight, take your problem to the only One who can really help you. Then, do what God puts it into your heart to do, and leave the rest to Him."

David promised to take her advice.

They spent a quiet week-end, visiting Ping in hospital, where he was trying to keep cheerful in spite of the weakness of his limbs. Early on Monday morning, David took his departure, his face pale, but resolved.

"I have been praying, Mum, and now I know that the only thing to do is to turn down Mr. Moore's offer. Esther will be disappointed. She might have nothing more to do with me! But with a mother like you and a sister like Trudy, I must do what is right."

Mrs. Lawson was greatly relieved, "You will not be sorry, David," she told him.

A few days later David wrote:

> "Well, folk, the deed is done and I have given Mr. Moore my decision. Esther was naturally disappointed, but—bless her!—she agrees with me that I mustn't bury my talent. She will wait, she says—no matter how long. Isn't she a great girl?"

"Yes," observed Mrs. Lawson when she got the letter. "Esther is worthy of David, and he is worthy of her. I only hope that when your turn comes, Trudy, you will be as happy in your choice of partner."

Trudy was amused. "Oh, Mum, that won't be for ages! I've simply no time for sweet-hearting, even if there was anybody."

But her mother smiled wisely. "Your time will come!" she declared.

* * * * *

One day Miss Bone was mysteriously absent from school.

"She lives alone, you know," Mr. Morison confided in Trudy, who was trying to teach the two classes together with the partition pushed back. "I'm rather worried about her. Anything might have happened."

Trudy agreed. "I know where she lives, Mr. Morison. I'll call in at lunch time."

The lonely villa with tall trees darkening the windows looked very forbidding, and Trudy felt a shudder as she rang the front door bell. It echoed through the house bringing no reply, so she went round to the back door. A bottle of milk was lying untouched on the step and still there was no answer to her summons.

Now she was quite sure that Miss Bone must be ill, but what was she to do? Greatly daring, she turned the handle and to her surprise found the door unlocked. She stepped into the old-fashioned scullery, all cluttered up with dishes and other utensils and through into the living-room which, though crowded with furniture, seemed very comfortless. The fireplace was full of ashes and the atmosphere stuffy. She called—

"Miss Bone, are you there?" but no reply came.

Then she tiptoed through the house opening door after door. There were plenty of them, and masses of dusty furniture in every room. It looked as if Miss Bone had inherited it from countless ancestors in the past. At last, upstairs, she came upon a small, dingy room with curtained windows. In the dimness she could make out a bed with somebody in it, and went nearer. Yes, it was Miss Bone, but her cheeks were fevered and she looked quite unlike herself.

"Miss Bone? I hope you don't mind my coming in, but I got no answer to my ring and the door was open. You look ill." She put a cool hand on the fevered forehead.

The invalid mumbled a request for water, and Trudy ran to fetch it. As she spooned it between the parched lips she asked:

"Who is your doctor? I'll have to fetch him."

She was relieved to learn that the Lawson family doctor also attended Miss Bone, and went along to the kiosk at the corner to phone him. Fortunately he was at home and promised to come immediately.

As well as she could, she tidied the patient and the room where she was lying. Living alone, Miss Bone seemed to have stopped caring about what things looked like. She was too dazed to make any objection to Trudy's ministrations and hardly seemed to know who she was.

"She's a queer one," was the doctor's confidential remark, as he was leaving the house after seeing the invalid. "She won't allow anyone into the house to work for her. Gloats over those old sticks of furniture like a miser. It's not good for a person to live alone in a big house like this."

"Is she very ill?" enquired Trudy.

"Bad enough. A sharp attack of 'flu, but the worst will soon be over, though if you had not come, it might have been a different story! She has no friends, you see."

"I know," Trudy told him. "She lived for her old mother and now that she's gone, she seems to have lost heart. Unfortunately, I've got to go back to school, but I'll let my mother know about her. She will come round, I'm sure."

"Ay, your mother is a good Samaritan if ever there was one. We can leave things in her hands."

Mrs. Lawson certainly proved herself a friend in need to Miss Bone. She and Trudy attended her constantly during the next week or two. On the first evening that the sick woman was allowed downstairs, she found a bright fire and touches of comfort in the living room that had not been there for years. Mrs. Lawson helped her into a chair.

"There now, don't talk if you don't want to. The doctor said you could stay up for an hour, but if you feel like going back to bed, just say so."

While in bed, Miss Bone had not spoken much at all. In a prim sort of way she thanked them when they did things for her, but giving the impression that the sooner they were gone the happier she would be. To-night, however, as she leaned back against the cushion which had been brought from the Lawson home, she lost some of her stiffness.

"This is kind of you, Mrs. Lawson. You shouldn't worry about me. I'm only a cranky old school teacher."

Mrs. Lawson smiled. "But you have been ill and need attention, Miss Bone."

At that the other melted completely. "I wish I had died!" she quavered.

A soothing hand was laid on hers. "Don't, please. It is wrong to wish that. God may be keeping you for some purpose of His own."

She shook a disbelieving head. "God? He has forsaken me long ago. Yet there was a time when he was good to me. I was happy and hopeful. Life was worth living, then!"

Mrs. Lawson said encouragingly: "If I can help you, just tell me, Miss Bone. It will do you good to get things off your mind."

The floodgates were opened. "Oh, how I have longed to tell someone! But I had no friends—my own fault, I know. Mrs. Lawson, I have been nursing a grudge against life for many years. It has made me bitter."

Then she went on to tell her story. How, on the eve of her marriage to a fine young man, her mother had become an incurable invalid. She gave up her fiancé to nurse her and he had married someone else. The iron had eaten into her soul and though she had given her mother devoted attention the rest of the world had been shut out. Even God had been shut out.

Mrs. Lawson pressed her hand. "It's not too late, you know. You can get rid of that sense of grudge.

Has it not eased you a little, speaking to me about it?"

"Yes, it has. I do feel better," she admitted.

"Then it will do you far more good to do what you ought to have done long ago," and she repeated softly words that were true not only for this poor sufferer, but for a multitude of others—

'Oh what peace we often forfeit!
Oh what needless pain we bear!
All because we do not carry
Everything to God in prayer.'

Miss Bone listened in silence. "It would be very difficult for me to pray," she said.

"Then I shall do it for you." Mrs. Lawson got down on her knees, calmly and sincerely as she did everything, and in simple words told God of her friend's troubles and commended her to His keeping.

Miss Bone closed her eyes and the tears flowed down her cheeks, but a new hope was born in her heart.

"Learn to open your heart to God, Miss Bone," advised the other. "Tell Him everything. You will find peace, and life will have a meaning it never had before."

CHAPTER XII

A VISIT FROM AN OLD FRIEND

PING was getting stronger, but progress was slow. With help, he could move about a little, but when it came to trying for himself, his legs failed him. In hospital they had done what they could for him and now he was to be allowed home, in the hope that the atmosphere there would encourage him to walk.

So once again the ambulance came to the gate of "Ardenlea" and Ping was carried into the room which was waiting for him. He was happy to see it again and to have Trudy and his mother fussing round him, but as he sat in the arm chair looking out to the rockery, his eyes became dreamy and sad.

"Nancy said when the spring came I would be out there, but it's spring now and here I am still, having to stay put."

Trudy understood how he felt, for 'hope deferred maketh the heart sick.'

"Cheer up, Ping. On the first warm day you will get out there to sit. If you only had a wheel chair, we could take you for walks."

"And let all the boys see me being wheeled about —no thank you!"

But Trudy had some money saved up from her salary and one day a simple type of wheel chair arrived for Ping. At first he refused to sit in it, but at last they persuaded him and Trudy pushed him the whole length of Lester Avenue. His self-consciousness faded as he saw how pleased people were to see him. He was treated as a kind of hero by his friends and by-and-by they took him further afield. The outings gave him an interest, and the fresh air was good for him, so that he became stronger in himself, though his legs still refused to work.

Sometimes Tom MacTavish came home with Trudy from school to take Ping out. The big, clumsy boy was infinitely gentle with the invalid and they became fast friends.

Then one day a letter came for Trudy which caused some excitement. It was from Brian Clyde, informing them that he had made arrangements to run a week's mission in Drumleigh and would take up his quarters in the field at Penny Farm where he had been before.

"So keep a lookout for the blue caravan, now rather the worse of wear,. but still good for a few thousand miles!"

Before it arrived, bills went up in the town advertising the visit of the 'Preaching Artist' and his wife, the well-known singer. Trudy told the boys in her class about them and urged them to go to the meetings. In fact, she broadcast the news wherever she went. She remembered that on their last visit Brian and Olivia had done much good in the town, and it was the least she could do to ensure that they got good audiences.

Late one afternoon, when Trudy and Ping were returning from an outing, the blue and fawn caravan passed them and stopped at the gate. Brian and Olivia both alighted and came to meet them.

Trudy felt the same thrill as she had done that wonderful summer at Ardensheel when she had met them for the first time.

Olivia had been sad then, for she had lost her voice and life seemed not worth living. Then Brian had appeared to help her across some stepping stones over a whirling stream. From that moment the fear in Olivia's heart was stilled. With Brian's help she came to know and to love the Christ he preached. Her voice was restored and when she married Brian she used it to help him in his great work.

Wonderful people, both! thought Trudy. Brian, tall and broad-shouldered with tanned face and crisp fair hair; Olivia tall too, but dark and gracefully slender.

The latter's soft eyes regarded Ping with compassion, but she greeted him brightly and Brian as usual was teasing in his sallies.

"'Schoolma'am Trudy', eh? We'll have to watch our P's and Q's, Olivia!"

"But I leave my schoolm'amishness behind at four o'clock," Trudy informed them

Brian laid a hand on Ping's shoulder. There was something rather remarkable about Brian's hands. Strong and sinewy, they yet had a delicacy of touch, and were able to transfer some of his own strength and personality, Ping felt this strength seeping into him now, just as Olivia had done on the stepping stones, and he looked up with adoration into the strong, smiling face, above him.

"Oh, Mr. Brian, I'm so glad you've come!"

"You have been through the doldrums, Ping, old fellow, but we'll pull you out, never fear!"

By this time Mrs. Lawson was out at the gate, insisting that they come in and have tea. Nancy was at home, too. They needed someone to play at the meetings and she thought she could get permission. After tea, Olivia tried over some solos with her at the piano and Ping enjoyed the rehearsal more than any.

"It's so long since I was able to go anywhere. I do wish I could come to one of your meetings!" he exclaimed.

"Why not?" asked Trudy. "I'll take you along in your chair. There will be room, won't there, Brian?"

"Certainly. Of course you must come, Ping. Everybody must come!"

They made plans to go to the first meeting of all. Brian had taken a bigger hall this time, the biggest in Drumleigh. MacTavish insisted on wheeling Ping's chair, and sat at the end of a row beside him. Trudy sat next to MacTavish with Miss Bone on her other side. The prim little school teacher was now showing a more friendly attitude, not only to Trudy but to the rest of the staff. But you could see there was still some inner conflict going on. Though Mrs. Lawson had kept in touch with her, she had never been able to break down her reserve again. Was she sorry now that she had bared her heart so completely? Surely not, when she had accepted Trudy's invitation to come to the meeting tonight.

Big as the hall was, it was crowded long before

starting time. All sorts of people were here—old and young, rich and poor, happy and sad. Just like the kind of crowd Jesus himself would have gathered, thought Trudy. Some had come out of curiosity, others from real need. Some already knew God, but to a great many He was a stranger.

When the platform party took its place, a hush fell over the assembly. After the chairman had introduced the two visitors to the town, Brian took over the meeting, and from the first moment he gripped the attention of his vast audience.

The first hymn they sang was that great song of praise—

> 'To God be the glory, great things He hath done—
> So loved He the world that He gave us His Son—'

and when the joyful strains had died away, he prayed for the assembled meeting and for humanity everywhere.

As the meeting went on Trudy felt very uplifted and happy, as if everyone here were being borne up on wings into another kind of world, a world of peace and light. Especially did she feel this while Olivia was singing the beautiful hymn: 'It is well, it is well with my soul.'

When the time came for Brian to deliver his Message, he stood for a moment in silence confronting them, this tall, manly preacher whose presence had a hidden power, because God was speaking through him.

"My friends," he began, "you heard these words which have just been sung—'It is well with my soul'.

Tonight I want to ask each one of you a question. Is it well with *your* soul?"

He paused, and with penetrating gaze seemed to scan each face, see into every heart. "If, as you sit there you feel that all is *not* well, let me tell you why.

"In the beginning man was created in the image of God, to be happy and sinless and to share in the glory of God. But man sinned. He disobeyed God. In his pride, he thought he knew better than God.

"Then God was angry and punished man. 'From now on,' he said, 'man will know sorrow and death, and he will be bowed down under the weight of his wickedness'."

His voice, stern and grave, held them tensely as he went on—"And so mankind laboured on without joy, without hope, just as some of you are labouring to-day. And there would still be no hope for any one of us, had not God also been a God of love. He looked down upon sinful, striving man and was filled with compassion for his foolish ways. Then in His mercy, He decided to give him a Second Chance."

Another pause while expectant faces were raised towards him—

"'I shall send My Son to earth,' He said, 'and He will give man a Message from Me. Those who receive Him, who listen to His word and give Him their hearts, I will take them again into My Kingdom. For them there will be no more death. They will find comfort in their sorrow and pardon for their sins.'"

Tenderly he smiled down upon his audience, holding out his arms towards them—

"This, then, is the Message from God. Take Jesus Christ into your life. Turn your heart from worldly things and give it into His keeping. Accept the Second Chance that a loving God has given you!"

Still they waited.

"My friends, I ask you, is it well with your soul? Is there within you a deep unrest, a feeling of frustration and defeat? Are you finding out as life goes on, that nothing gives you real satisfaction—not money, not possessions, not any form of earthly pleasure?"

He paused dramatically, then continued in ringing tones—"There is a cure for all this sickness of soul! All those troubles lying so heavily on your life are the result of man's original sin. Get rid of them! Unburden yourselves and go out from this meeting place free men, free women!"

A tremor went through his audience as he resumed:

"This cure that is so simple, so miraculous, can be yours tonight. This is *your* moment of decision. The choice lies before you now. You can decide to reject Christ and remain in your darkness, or you can accept Him and come into the Light!"

Now his voice became soft and pleading. "Come, then! Come forward here to me now, while we pray together. Do not be afraid to declare your decision. You will give encouragement and heart to those who are still undecided. Come then, my friends, wherever you are, whoever you are. To-night God is speaking to you, and he says—Come!"

There was no sound at first as they bowed their heads in silent prayer. Then Trudy heard a rustling of footsteps, hesitant, then becoming steadier, louder, like a rising wind, as one after another rose from their seats and went forward to the front of the platform.

Though Trudy had made her own decision years ago in prayer by her bedside, she re-dedicated herself in her heart as these others made their resolve for the first time.

During Brian Clyde's appeal she had felt Miss Bone sitting very stiffly and tensely by her side. Now she gave a nervous little cough and shifted about uneasily. Trudy gave her arm a reassuring squeeze and with a jerk Miss Bone got to her feet and passing to the end of the row, went to join the others at the front. Tears sprang to Trudy's eyes. Full well she knew what courage had been required to make the move. Her mother's prayers, then, had not been in vain.

But Tom MacTavish was pulling her sleeve. "Miss," he said in a husky whisper, "I want to go forward too, but I don't like."

She said, "Go, Tom. God will give you courage."

To her joy he got up at once, and his big boots clattered down the passage, to be followed by more footsteps as others of her class rose to follow MacTavish to the front. She knew a great thankfulness. Whatever lay before these boys in the future, they would always have tonight's experience to guide them. She was glad that she had prepared them for this decision in the Bible lessons at school, so that the seed had fallen on fertile ground.

Olivia had begun to sing. Like a silver thread of

sound, the pleading words came to their waiting ears—

'Softly and tenderly Jesus is calling,
Calling for you and for me,
See, on the portals He's waiting and watching,
Watching for you and for me—'

Then came Brian's voice again—"Jesus is saying, 'Come' . . . There is still time to answer that call . . ."

Trudy had not forgotten about Ping, who was sitting quietly in his wheel chair with MacTavish's empty seat between them. She looked at him now and saw that his eyes were shining and his hands were pressed down on the arms of his chair as if he were trying to rise. While she watched, she saw to her amazement that he actually had risen—he was on his feet! She started to his side, but he said firmly—

"No, Trudy, I can walk by myself!" and he began to take slow but steady steps forward, until on reaching the platform, still with his eyes on Brian Clyde's face, he held out his hands, and the preacher took them in his strong ones and held them fast.

CHAPTER XIII

PING WALKS AGAIN

IT was gloriously true. Ping could walk. Though exhausted when they got him home, he was able to show them again what he could do.

"I suddenly seemed to get strength," he said. "Brian was holding out his hands and when he said —'Jesus says "Come",' I knew he meant me. So I went."

It was all as simple as that.

People got to know about Ping's wonderful recovery and the doctors who had attended him were amazed. Their skill had been effective so far, but it needed an extra 'plus'—Ping's complete faith in God—to make the cure perfect.

So successful was their mission that Brian and Olivia stayed in Drumleigh for an extra week. After that they moved on to Martonbury for a fortnight's mission there.

There was a stirring among the people whose hearts had so long been turned away from God. They were tired of their little pleasures, the aimless round, the 'getting and spending'. They wanted something real, something to give them assurance in days of foreboding, when the whole of mankind seemed in danger of destruction. And what better assurance was there than the one that 'Jesus saves'?

Day by day Ping made more progress, and one bright morning he betook himself off to school, full of happy anticipation, so different from the unwilling schoolboy of the past!

One evening about this time, Mr. Moore called to see them. Trudy opened the door to him and noticed that he looked more haggard than ever—

"Haven't you been well, Mr. Moore?" she enquired anxiously.

"It makes me feel better just to look at your bright face," was the reply. "May I see your mother for a few minutes?"

Many people came to consult her mother about their troubles and Trudy never obtruded, so she showed him into the room and left them together. They had not seen much of Mr. Moore lately, for he had avoided them since his refusal to let Esther and David be engaged.

Trudy recalled the occasion years ago, when her mother had come to Mr. Moore's rescue. It was the time when Esther ran away from home because of his indifference and hardness of heart. When they found her she was very ill, practically dying, and her father, knowing himself to blame, was tortured beyond endurance.

Soon, however, he was on his knees beside Mrs. Lawson. On that day he had vowed to let the love of God into his heart, to begin life anew. Trudy had begun to wonder lately if he had forgotten that hour of stress, for when a man's days were solely occupied with the making of money, it was easy for him to forget higher things.

Mrs. Lawson had wondered the same thing. When she greeted Andrew Moore this evening, she sensed immediately that this man was again in need of help.

"Sit down, Mr. Moore. How nice to see you again. But you don't look well. You must take better care of yourself!"

He took a chair, heaving a sigh. "The very atmosphere of this house is comforting. Mrs. Lawson, I hope you will forgive me for taking up your time, but there is something on my mind."

She gave him an encouraging smile. "Then I am glad you have decided to get it off."

"I could not do it with anyone but you. You have been a good friend to me, Mrs. Lawson, and I have done nothing in return."

"Friends do not ask for return, Mr. Moore," she said quietly.

He smiled. "I am afraid I am too used to people who extort their last 'drop of blood'. Mrs. Lawson, yesterday I went to see a heart specialist. He told me what I have been suspecting; that I have heart trouble. I shall have to take things easy in future."

She leant forward in sympathy—"Oh, Mr. Moore, I am so sorry!"

He replied, shading his eyes with a shaking hand, "Thank you, I know you are sincere. It seems I may live for quite a long time. On the other hand, death may come upon me quite suddenly. That thought, Mrs. Lawson, had made me see how trivial are the things I have been setting store by."

There was a short, tense silence before he went on.

"Years ago you pointed out to me that one should not lay up 'treasures on earth, where moth and dust doth corrupt.' I have been forgetting that. My feet have strayed from the path you once set them on. I have been neglecting to pray, to read my Bible. I realised this one evening some time ago, when I attended one of Brian Clyde's meetings."

Her face brightened. "So you heard Brian Clyde? I'm so glad."

"God spoke to me through that man, but I paid no heed. Deliberately, I shut out the voice of God, but I got no peace! Then last night, knowing that my time on earth might be short, I yielded myself anew to Him."

Her eyes were wet. "You do feel happier, now?"

"Yes, Mrs. Lawson, I feel I can meet death calmly when it comes. But first I must undo some of the unhappiness I have caused."

"You mean, about Esther and David?"

He nodded. "You know how much I love my daughter. I knew of course that some day a husband would claim her. He would be no ordinary fellow, I vowed; only the best need apply! I thought in terms of worldly status, and your boy, Mrs. Lawson, did not come up to my demands."

Her eyes smiled into his. "He hasn't much money, but he is a good boy, Mr. Moore."

"I know that. At first when he turned down my offer to take him into the business, I was angry. Now, I realise that his standard of values is a high one, the highest there is. He is a son to be proud of, Mrs. Lawson; I take back all my objections. They may marry as soon as it can be arranged. I should like to see Esther happily settled before I have to go."

"I see." Mrs. Lawson spoke softly. "This will make them both very happy, Mr. Moore. Will you tell them soon?"

"I want you to do that," he said, rising. "I think you will be able to put it better than I can."

* * * * *

The opportunity came next day. David had come home for the week-end and Esther was expected for tea, though this was a secret to all but Mrs. Lawson. Even Trudy knew nothing about the reason for Mr. Moore's visit.

As usual, David was glad to be home. Though he loved his job, his lodgings were not very comfortable and his evenings were lonely. How he would appreciate a home of his own with Esther there to greet him when he came back from work!

Trudy was preparing tea when the bell rang. She put down the gas under the fish and went to answer it, but David got there first.

"It's Esther!" His face was glowing. "What a surprise!"

When she came in her first glance was for him.

"Yes, David. Dad specially wanted me home for the weekend, but he wouldn't tell me why. He is coming round later, Mrs. Lawson," she said to Trudy's mother, who had come to welcome the guest.

"I think I can tell you why your father wanted you, Esther."

She took the girl's hand and laid it in David's. Then she stood back and smiled at them.

"There! She is yours, David. Her father has given her to you." She would not spoil their happiness by mentioning Mr. Moore's illness. Plenty of time for that later.

"So that was why Esther's father came!" exclaimed Trudy. "To tell you this, to get you to break the news. Isn't it wonderful?"

David and Esther were regarding each other with shining eyes. Her cheeks were flushed, her lips smiling and tremulous. "Dad was so sweet to me to-day, I began to wonder—Oh, David!"

"Esther!" he breathed and took her in his arms before them all.

At that moment Ping came on the scene with Rusty at his heels. He was looking the picture of health.

"What's all this? David hugging Esther—in public!"

"They're engaged," explained Trudy. "They're going to be married!"

"Oh, I see." To a boy of thirteen, it was rather a needless fuss. David had always been soppy about Esther, anyone might have guessed they would get married one of those days.

"Congrats, David, Esther's a grand girl. She would have to be to put up with you!"

David only laughed. He was right on top of the world and nothing could down him.

Then they went in to have tea. Nancy joined them before it was over. What a gabble of tongues there was, what reminiscences from the past! Remember the wee pansy brooch? they said—

and lo and behold there it was fastened in Esther's blouse.

"It was only a cheap thing," said David. "The ring I buy you will be worth more than that."

"No." Esther fingered the brooch lovingly. "The most expensive ring in the world could never mean more than this to me."

"I am never going to marry," put in Nancy. "Nursing is too important. I'm going to wed myself to my profession."

They laughed. "I've always noticed," said David, "that girls that vow not to marry are always the first to go off. What about you, Trudy?"

"Someday I might, but not for ages and ages. At present I think girls are much nicer than men."

At last Ping interrupted with—"Can't you talk about something else? Marrying is awfully dull!"

Mrs. Lawson smiled at her youngest. He would soon grow up too and go out into the world of men and women. She expected great things of Ping, now that he had been restored to health and strength.

"And by the way," he went on, "now that we're all together and everybody is listening, perhaps I can get my oar in. It's about that name, 'Ping'. It's not my real name and it sounds sort of babyish. I'm nearly a man now and I'll be obliged, everybody, if you'll call me 'Peter'."

Consternation in the family. "But," objected Nancy, "we simply couldn't! It wouldn't be you."

"He's quite right," declared his mother. "He deserves his real name and we must make an effort."

There were grumbles. They would never remember, they said.

Gradually, however, they did remember, and 'Peter' it was. But to his mother the old name 'Ping' was the sweetest one, and was to remain so in her memory.

* * * * *

Now it was summer and getting near the school holidays. The big event in July was to be the wedding, with Trudy as bridesmaid and Derek Crawford as 'best man.'

But before the wedding came the final day at school and the end of Trudy's first year as a teacher.

In the forenoon lessons were supposed to be carried on as usual, but the boys were restless and excited and at last she gave up trying to revise the geography of Australia. Surely on this last day she could forsake the timetable for once.

"Well, then," she told them, "it seems you are not interested in geography, so we'll talk about something nearer home. Quite a number of you are leaving school to-day. Some are going to be engineers, others to work in factories, some in shops and some in offices."

The school leavers sat up straight, looking very important.

"I don't want you to forget your schooldays," she went on. "A lot of what you have learned will be thrown to the winds, I know. But do remember some things, please. I want you all to make up your minds to practise what I've told you about being a Christian. It won't be easy for some of you. People will tempt you to do wrong things. But you mustn't yield. If you have Christ as your Saviour He will help you, and keep you. Now, who are the ones who are going to be brave and stand up for the right?"

She looked round the earnest faces. "Have you got the courage to stand up?"

The first one to spring to his feet was MacTavish. Then followed the ones who had gone forward with him at Brian Clyde's meeting. Soon practically the whole class was standing. They were still on their feet when Mr. Morison opened the door and came in.

"Well, Miss Lawson, everybody looks very earnest in here! Are you putting them on their honour?"

"That is just what I am doing," and she told him what had brought the boys to their feet. He addressed them with a smile—

"I am glad to hear that you boys are courageous enough to make a promise like that to your teacher. And let me tell you, you are very fortunate chaps to have a teacher like Miss Lawson for your last year at school. I hope you agree with me?"

"Yes, sir!" was the whole-hearted acclamation.

He proceeded to give them a practical talk about what lay before them, to which they listened with perfect attention. He then confided to Trudy that he might see his way next session to hold a weekly service as she had suggested.

"On thinking it over, I don't see any harm in

letting something else go by the board. First things first, as you so aptly reminded me."

This was something she had not anticipated, a minor triumph which made her very happy. She thanked him, and he had hardly gone from the room before MacTavish rose importantly to his feet, his face very red, his hair looking more carroty than ever.

"Please Miss," he began, swallowing nervously, "I mean—Miss Lawson, ladies and gentlemen—no, just gentlemen—" and he bowed to the class, "it is my pleasant duty on this last day of the term to thank you, Miss, for all your kind teaching and even for the punishment exercises you have given us."

He paused, and the class applauded.

"That's nice of you," replied Trudy. "Are you finished, now?"

"No, Miss, I've just started." He cleared his throat. "Thank you, too, for not belting us—I mean, for not using the tawse. It would have deserved us right if you had."

"'Served us right'" corrected Trudy.

"Yes, Miss. To show you, Miss, how much we think of you, we would like to give you a—a mark of our esteem—" really, MacTavish was a budding orator—"and it is now my pleasant duty—no, I said that before. It is now my privilege, Miss, to present you with this gift from the boys of 5B."

He clattered to the floor and handed her a small parcel. Inside was a red box which she opened to disclose a shiny black fountain pen. Very moved by it all, she took out the pen for a closer look while they waited expectantly.

"Thank you, MacTavish. Thank you, boys. I never expected a present from you, especially a present like this. Every time I use this pen, I shall think of the boys of 5B and the kindness which prompted them to give it to me."

MacTavish cleared his throat again. "Three cheers for Miss Lawson!"

The cheers came with noise and vigour. Trudy felt sorry for Miss Bone next door.

In the afternoon the whole school was assembled in the central hall for a puppet show given by Trudy's boys. It was an unqualified success and all concerned were covered in glory, puppets and their manipulators alike. Even Miss Bone was won over at last. Not that she would ever teach puppetry herself, for she was due to retire from teaching, and would be leaving Balfour St. for good.

Trudy accompanied her home that day. "You will come and see us during the holidays, Miss Bone?"

"Certainly." Outwardly she was still a little prim. "Your mother has been very good to me, Miss Lawson. But for her and you, I would still be an unhappy woman."

"You are feeling better than you were, then?" But there was no need to ask, Miss Bone looked ten years younger, and people had ceased to shun her.

"I found the answer to my problems that night at Brian Clyde's meeting. It was then I became quite convinced that your mother was right, that I would not be free until I surrendered my heart to God. Now, I am putting my old life behind me forever.

Even at sixty-five it is not impossible to begin anew!"

She had sold the old house, she told Trudy, and had bought a small cottage a few miles out in the country.

"I have lived too long with the ghosts of the past. All that old furniture has been sold off—what a relief! You must come and see me some day when I am settled."

Trudy promised gladly.

"There's a family of young people next door," the other informed her. "They seem very pleasant and I'm sure I shall like them."

"Making up your mind to like new people is half the battle," remarked Trudy.

"Yes, and the opposite holds good. For too long now, I have looked on new people as potential enemies, especially young people. That was the surest way to make them enemies, of course. You were the exception; you kept friendly in spite of everything. Thank you, my dear."

That walk home with Miss Bone seemed a perfect ending to a school year of ups-and-downs that she could not possibly have foretold. Truly, one lived and learned. She had once thought that a teacher must surely know everything there was to know. How wrong she had been!

CHAPTER XIV

AN END AND A BEGINNING

ON the morning of the wedding Trudy awoke very early and lay for a while thinking over the events of the past year. Yes, it was exactly a year since Esther and she had left college. On that day, their ways had parted, but now a bigger separation was to come about. Esther would leave her girlhood days behind for ever. Instead of Esther Moore, she would be 'Mrs. David Lawson'. She would move into a world of new experience, leaving Trudy behind.

Oh well, reflected Trudy, there was time enough to dwell on that later. The days' events would be too crowded for regrets, and after all a wedding was a time for rejoicing, wasn't it?

Now she could hear her mother stirring, and sprang out of bed to put on the kettle for an early cup of tea. The wedding was to be at two o'clock in Esther's house. Owing to Mr. Moore's health, it was to be a quiet occasion. To their joy, Brian Clyde had promised to officiate at the ceremony and Olivia would be there too. Then there would be the two families with their close friends, and the Crawfords from Martonbury, whose train Trudy was to meet in the forenoon.

At the station, watching the train steam in, she wondered if there would be any change in the Crawfords since their last meeting. There they were, coming towards her now. Mr. and Mrs. Crawford had not changed a bit, but Derek seemed older, surely?

She looked at him with interest. He was not exactly what you would call good-looking. His nose, for instance, was not the perfect feature David's was, and his face was too thin and serious looking. But even as she looked, she saw his expression change as he flashed her a smile. What a transformation! He looked really handsome, now.

They all shook hands. "You're a fine one," said Derek. "You never answered my letter."

Trudy apologised. "And now I don't need to, do I?" she asked.

"Certainly you do! I'm not letting you off with it. How is the prospective bridegroom?" he enquired gaily.

"Oh, he's in a hopeless state of nerves, I'm so glad you are here to take care of him!"

"I'll see the ring isn't lost, trust me. I've married off three brothers, you know. I've seen enough of weddings to put me off them for life."

His mother's eyes twinkled. "Don't believe him; Derek loves weddings."

At Ardenlea, they found things rather disorganised. While Mrs. Lawson was preparing refreshments for the guests, Nancy and Peter—alias Ping—were quarrelling as to who should get into the bathroom first.

"I'm a girl and need more time to dress than you!" declared Nancy.

"But my new kilt takes years to put on! There's

about fifty different pieces. A girl's frock is a simple matter!" was the retort.

David settled the argument by ordering them both to wait.

"Without me there can't be a wedding at all. You'll get the bathroom when *I* am finished with it, and that's that!"

* * * * *

Trudy had to leave them to go to Esther's, where she would put on her bridesmaid's frock and help the bride to dress. At the last minute she had to sew on a button for Nancy and polish Ping's buckle shoes, but she got away at last.

Esther was all ready but for her wedding gown. Both girls were too excited to take any of the lunch offered them by the housekeeper. From the bed Trudy lifted carefully the gown of white satin and lace. It was simply cut, with long tapered sleeves, Esther's only adornment being a string of pearls.

"There!" Having fastened it up, Trudy stood back to admire. "We'll fix the veil after I put on my own frock. A year ago, when we graduated, I thought how lovely you looked in white, Esther. I didn't know then how soon I'd be seeing you as a bride!"

"Do I look all right for David?" was all Esther could think about.

"All right? I never saw such a beautiful bride; I don't believe there ever was one. Now, sit down and don't move! You're liable to crush something."

While Esther sat very stately and still, she donned the shell pink silk frock which had been chosen for her bridesmaid's outfit.

"Some day you will be a bride too," commented her friend. "You'll invite me to your wedding? I can be your 'matron of honour!'"

"Thanks, I'll let you know in plenty of time. Can you wait ten years or so?" she asked.

"I don't think it will be as long as that. Oh, Trudy I'm so happy! I never dreamed anyone could be so happy as this. God is good to me. Every minute of my life I will be grateful to Him."

Some girls in her place would have taken happiness for granted, but not so Esther. She felt that she was specially blest, and must make return for what she had received. Had she not the best and truest of men to love her and the kindest of fathers to give his blessing to their union? Mr. Moore had been very generous in his wedding gift, a new bungalow on the outskirts of Martonbury, to which they would go on return from their honeymoon. He had promised to visit them often, for he was retiring from business.

"I think Dad looks better already, don't you?" was Esther's next remark.

Trudy agreed. "It's seeing you so happy that makes him happy too, and our feelings affect our health."

"I know. That time I ran away from home—remember?—and had that mysterious illness, it was all due to feeling miserable."

"The same with Ping—Peter, I mean. He got

so down in the mouth he just couldn't get better. But Brian Clyde came and gave him hope. Faith worked a miracle in him that night."

Now it was time to put on Esther's wedding veil, a precious heirloom from her mother, who had been married in it a quarter of a century ago. Hardly had Trudy adjusted it, than Mr. Moore knocked at the door to say it was time to go downstairs, and to give them the flowers they were to carry, white lilies for Esther, pink carnations for Trudy.

Trudy, who had never been at a wedding before, was very impressed and deeply moved at what followed.

First, they sang the 23rd Psalm—'The Lord's my Shepherd, I'll not want'; then came a prayer and later the solemn marriage ceremony.

She stood near to Esther, ready to take her bouquet when required, and Derek was there too doing his duty as 'best man'.

Now came the point when David put the ring on his bride's finger—'With this ring I thee wed'. How his hand shook while he was doing it! But Esther smiled encouragingly—she did not seem in the least nervous—and Trudy realised that now they were man and wife.

The closing hymn was, she thought, the loveliest she had ever heard in her life.

> 'O perfect love, all human thought transcending,
> Lowly we kneel in prayer before Thy throne,
> That theirs may be the love which knows no ending
> Whom Thou for evermore dost join in one.'

Looking round at the people gathered here,

whom she knew so well, she noticed that they seemed transformed. It was not only that they wore fine clothes. Their faces were radiant too, as if they were sharing in the high happiness of the bride and groom.

Then, after the register had been signed, what a crowding round of guests, with kisses and congratulations!

During the excitement Trudy heard Ping's voice at her elbow. "This is all very well, True, but when does the food come on? I'm starvishing!" The old expression seemed to make him a lovable little boy again.

Trudy realised that she was 'starvishing' too, but fortunately the wedding lunch was announced and they all went into the big dining-room which had been taken over by a catering firm. There Ping enjoyed the meal of his life, which he was to boast of for months afterwards.

Now that the strain was past, Esther and David, flushed and sparkling, joined in the fun. Speeches were made. Derek proposed a toast 'to the bride' with such wit and humour that he had everyone laughing. Certainly this quiet young man had more social assets than Trudy had imagined!

Afterwards in the lounge they gathered round the piano while Olivia sang solos and the others joined in the choruses. Then, at a signal from Derek, Trudy took Esther upstairs to help her change into her 'going-away' costume.

Off came the wedding veil and the lovely satin gown, to be replaced by a suit of pale grey with a straw hat to match trimmed with pink rosebuds. All ready, Esther turned to Trudy, hugging her very tightly, a mist in her blue eyes.

"I can't thank you enough and I'm not going to try to! Remember, you're still my best friend. I'll write to you, Trudy, we'll both write!"

David was waiting for her on the landing while Derek kept watch. The car that was taking them away had slid up to the gate and they hoped to get away without being seen. Derek crept downstairs with the suit cases and David and Esther followed, hand in hand.

But their precautions were in vain. A door suddenly opened and the guests came surging out.

"Come on! Run for it!" David pulled Esther towards the door. But Ping got there first. Showers of confetti were sprayed upon the happy couple until, breathless, they reached the shelter of the car and the door was shut.

Standing on the steps, Trudy saw two radiant faces, hands waving a farewell, and more rainbow showers of confetti as the car was driven away.

Then, as it turned the corner and disappeared, a hush fell, and everybody looked at each other as if not knowing what to do next. The highlight of the day had faded, leaving everything flat and dull.

Trudy suddenly felt terribly lonely; she gave a sigh, so tiny she was sure no one would hear. But someone did hear it. He was standing by her side, his dark eyes on her face.

"Don't be sad, Trudy! They've gone away, but they'll come back again."

"Yes, Derek, but it will never be the same."

Derek's gay smile flashed out. "Nothing stays the same. Who would want it to? But the end of one thing means the beginning of something else. Don't think about losing; think about finding!"

He took her arm gallantly to lead her indoors and she smiled back at him, comforted.